Library and Information Service

Library materials must be returned on or before the last date stamped or fines will be charged at the current rate. Items can be renewed online, by telephone, letter or personal call unless required by another borrower. For hours of opening and charges see notices displayed in libraries.

Lewisham Library
199/201 Lewisham High Street
London SE13 6LG

D1076766

Best Day Walks in **SNOWDONIA**

JOHN GILLHAM

F

FRANCES LINCOLN LIMITED
PUBLISHERS

**LEWISHAM
LIBRARY SERVICE**

Askews & Holts	20-Jul-2012
796.51	

Frances Lincoln Limited
4 Torriano Mews
Torriano Avenue
London NW5 2RZ

Best Day Walks in Snowdonia
Copyright © 2012 Frances Lincoln Limited

Text, photographs and 3D sketch maps
Copyright © 2012 John Gillham
Edited by Roly Smith
Designed by Jane Havell Associates Ltd
First Frances Lincoln edition 2012

John Gillham has asserted his moral right to be
identified as Author of this Work in accordance with
the Copyright, Designs and Patents Act 1988

Contains Ordnance Survey data
© Crown copyright and database right 2011

All rights reserved. No part of this publication
may be reproduced, stored in a retrieval system
or transmitted, in any form, or by any means,
electronic, mechanical, photocopying, recording
or otherwise, without either prior permission in
writing from the publishers or a licence permitting
restricted copying. In the United Kingdom such
licences are issued by the Copyright Licensing
Agency, Saffron House, 6–10 Kirby Street,
London EC1N 8TS

A catalogue record for this book is available from
the British Library

ISBN 978-0-7112-3253-2
Printed and bound in China
9 8 7 6 5 4 3 2 1

Frontispiece: The Dwyryd estuary and the Rhinogydd peaks seen from Moel y Gest.

ACKNOWLEDGEMENTS

I would like to thank Ronald Turnbull for being a jolly helpful friend,
my pal Roly Smith, a genial editor (as Ronald once said) and, last but not least,
my wife Nicola, who has been with me on the hills in all weathers

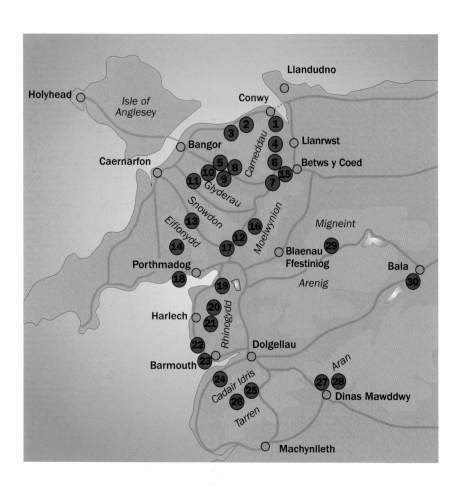

CONTENTS

INTRODUCTION

The high country of Wales reaches its zenith in the north-west corner, where the angular rock peaks rise into the sky, towering above the towns and villages of the valleys and coast. This is Snowdonia, or Eryri, as the Welsh know it. Snowdonia used to represent the area around the highest peak, Snowdon, the Glyderau, the Carneddau and Moel Siabod, but in 1951 the Snowdonia National Park was designated and its territory includes mountains as far south as Machynlleth and as far east as Bala.

Even the names of Snowdonia and Eryri have sparked controversy. Conventional wisdom had it that Snowdon is Saxon and meant snowy peak, so called because the frequently snow-covered landmark aided sailors returning to west coast ports. Eryri was supposed to mean the land of eagles – all very romantic, but fanciful. Much more likely is the theory by Sir Ifor Williams, who went back to the old Welsh term *eryr*, plural *eryri*, which simply meant highlands.

Today's national park, the third to be designated in Britain, covers 840 sq miles/ 2,176 sq km, and is home to 25,500 people. Its industries of slate quarrying and lead mining have mostly gone, with tourism taking their place. The tourists come to see the great mountain scenery, and Snowdonia has many spectacular ranges, with a diversity of landscape and vegetation.

In the north the Carneddau are great whalebacks, with long grassy ridges rising from Thomas Telford's Holyhead highway (the A5) to the north coast. On the other side of this road are the Glyderau – rugged and rough-cast, rather like a practice session for the great creation that is Snowdon, whose beautifully sculpted, lake-filled corries and perfect pyramidal summit massif have inspired artists and poets for centuries. The slate of the Moelwynion and the Eifionydd ranges has left them with a legacy of man's carvings rather than Nature's, and some of their lower slopes have been reduced to rubble. Yet still they rise above such things, with fine rocky ridges and high, lonely and unspoiled cwms.

Opposite: Storm over Snowdon.

The oldest of the Welsh mountain rocks, those of the Cambrian era some 500 million years ago, come to the surface on the Rhinogydd peaks. This range is favoured by the connoisseur and lies to the south of Tremadog Bay and the Llyn Peninsula. Its crags are gnarled and faulted, with only thin soils cloaked with heather. Here little paths, made by goats as much as people, lead walkers to wonderful corners where crag-bound lakes proliferate.

To the east of the range and the busy A470 stretches the Migneint, a great wilderness of peat bog, heather and moor grass. The Arenig mountain range looks down on this wilderness. Its highest summit, Arenig Fawr, is a twin-peaked colossus, with just enough rock architecture to keep things interesting and its own tarn sheltered by the eastern rock face. To the south its satellites, Dduallt and Rhobell Fawr, slip back into wilderness, an attractive area only slightly tempered by the spread of plantations of spruce and larch.

To the south, Cadair Idris and the Aran mountains complete the picture, along with the compact Tarren and Dyfi Hills, which lie in between.

Cadair is perhaps the most beautiful of Snowdonia's mountains, with the fine glacial form of Snowdon, but with magnificent surroundings of velvety, verdant valleys and the exquisite Mawddach estuary. The conifers of the Dyfi Forest have engulfed the Tarrens and the Dyfi Hills, but splendid walks are still possible in the places where the conifers cannot reach, and the remnants of the mining and quarrying industries offer fascinating insights into times gone by.

The Aran mountains rise in splendid mountain form from Cwm Cywarch near Dinas Mawddwy, with the main ridge spanning 10 miles/16 km before declining to the shores of Llyn Tegid (Bala Lake) at Llanuwchllyn. The range, which forms the southern boundary of the national park, has an ice-sculpted eastern face with cliffs, gullies and rocky bluffs and views into the lonely cwms, stretching into the anonymous but fascinating hillscapes of Mid Wales.

Using the book

Each of the 30 walks has been graded from one to five for both technical difficulty and strenuousness:

•	easy	••••	fairly difficult / strenuous
••	fairly easy	•••••	difficult / strenuous
•••	moderate		

None of the walks contains any difficult or exposed scrambling. The itineraries range from the easy-paced walk on the foothills above Bala to a steep rocky assault on Tryfan. Even here I have used the easiest routes of ascent and descent. By starting on the easier routes and working up through the grades, families and newcomers should gain a good introduction to mountain walking, as long as they learn how to use both map and compass, or GPS unit. Remember, though, to be aware of weather changes. The most amiable mountain can become a very dangerous place in adverse conditions such as snow, ice and high winds. A good book to learn these skills is *Navigation: Techniques and Skills for Walkers* by Pete Hawkins (Cicerone).

Remember, too, even the mountains change. A storm could have brought down a path across loose mountain scree or friable terrain; a bridge could have been washed away by those storms, or agricultural operations of some sort or another could have necessitated a diversion or closure of a path. River crossings can

Above: On the summit of Snowdon. This walk is rated •••• for technical difficulty and ••••• for strenuousness (see page 81).

become difficult or even impossible after periods of snow or heavy rainfall and conifer plantations are forever changing. Spruce trees reach maturity quickly and whole blocks are felled, leaving behind hard-to-follow or diverted footpaths. Always be prepared to adjust your itinerary.

Each walk is accompanied by a basic plan map and a 3D panoramic drawing. The former will allow you to transfer your route on to the relevant walkers' map, either Harvey's or Ordnance Survey Explorer, while the latter will give you a good idea of the terrain and the height gains and losses along the way. The 3D drawings are not to scale and occasionally I have used artistic licence to bring hidden detail into sight. The walk descriptions have numbered waypoints, which will help with map reading and route finding. To this end, the waypoints are annotated on both sets of maps.

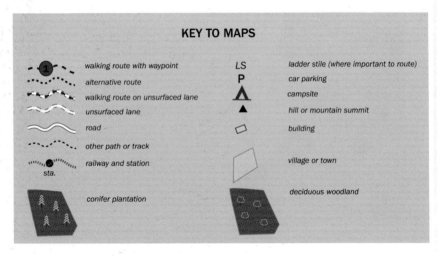

KEY TO MAPS

walking route with waypoint	*LS* — ladder stile (where important to route)
alternative route	P — car parking
walking route on unsurfaced lane	— campsite
unsurfaced lane	▲ — hill or mountain summit
road	— building
other path or track	
railway and station	— village or town
conifer plantation	— deciduous woodland

If you have a mind to extend or alter the routes, then the author's four-volume *Pictorial Guides to the Mountains of Snowdonia* (Frances Lincoln) will fit the bill. They are a complete guide to *all* the ascents of each of Snowdonia's mountains.

Opposite: Y Garn, one of the rugged Glyderau peaks.

CONWY MOUNTAIN, CASTLE AND COAST

Conwy is a magnificent town, and you'll want to take a good look around before taking to the hills. Three bridges, including Thomas Telford's wonderful suspension bridge of 1822, span the river beneath the mighty castle, allowing road and railway into this medieval World Heritage Site. The castle itself dates back to 1287. The powerful English king Edward I built it as part of his 'iron ring' to repress the Welsh troops of Llewelyn the Great. A statue of the revered Welsh prince dominates Lancaster Square in the heart of the town.

Great town walls 6 feet/2m thick and 35 feet/11m high with three original gates and numerous towers still encircle the old town, and the walkway along them offers fine rooftop views of the castle, the Conwy estuary and the quayside.

Conwy has many fine old buildings in the heart of the town within the walls. The half-timbered Aberconwy House has origins in the fourteenth century, although most of its structure dates to around 1500. This old merchant's house is now owned by the National Trust. Plas Mawr is a large restored mansion, built for the Wynne family in 1576. Now open to the public, the building has some fine interior plasterwork which was hidden for centuries in order to save it from destruction at the hands of the Cromwellian Puritans.

The Carneddau mountains rise from the town walls of Conwy, forming a low ridge, Mynydd y Dref, or Conwy Mountain as it is better known. The ridge, which forms the backbone of this walk, offers a splendid easy-striding promenade on firm stony paths through short grass, heather, stunted gorse and bilberry. On its highest point, 800ft/244m, stands Castell Caer Seion, a 10-acre/4-ha fort, which has been linked with both Iron Age and Roman settlers.

Opposite: Conwy from its town walls.

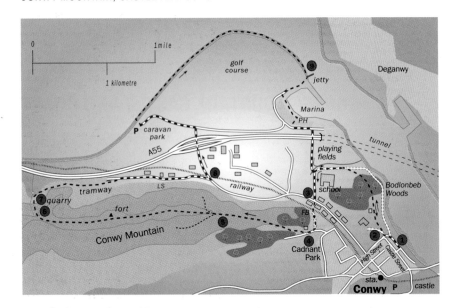

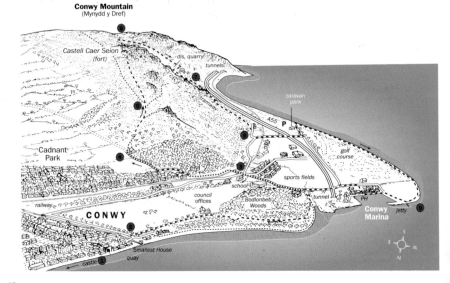

Distance 6½ miles / 11 km
Time 4 hours
Ascent 985ft / 300m
Technical difficulty •
Strenuousness ••
Map OS Explorer OL17 Snowdon
Start / finish Conwy Town Quay
(GR SH 782777). Car park at Morfa Bach,
Llanrwst Road (B5106)
Public toilets In the Morfa Bach car park; by
the start of the walk on the town quay (Lower
Gate); in the car park at the end of the road to
Conwy Morfa.

1 At the start of the walk by Lower Gate, the castle will be dominant overlooking the quayside, where fishermen may be tending their nets, watched by greedy seagulls. Pass in front of the Liverpool Arms, and the Smallest House, a tiny red-painted fisherman's cottage, before going through a gateway in the town walls, where the road and the walls turn left.

2 After a few paces turn right along a tarmac drive heading towards Bodlonbeb Woods. With the council offices on the left, take a right fork past gardens on the right. The tarred path becomes unsurfaced and climbs through the woods. Follow the outdoor challenge waymarkers, taking first a left fork, then a right turn at a T-junction of paths. The path soon descends to a gate by an information board. Through the gate you turn left on a tarred path (Marine Walk). Turn left along the road, past the school to the A547.

3 Cross the road, then go straight across into a cul-de-sac before crossing the coast railway on a footbridge. The track beyond skirts a wood to reach Mountain Road, where you turn right.

4 A waymarker by a house guides you on to a path on the right which, beyond a stile, rakes up hillside scattered with wind-twisted hawthorns. You are now high on Conwy Mountain's southern slopes. Ignore a North Wales Path waymarker pointing across these slopes; instead your route follows the path to the crest, from where you can gaze across Conwy Bay to the limestone isthmus of Llandudno's Great Orme and the flat plains of Anglesey.

5 There is quite a network of paths crisscrossing the undulating ridge, but stick with the highest to pass through the remains of Castell Caer Lleion.

6 Beyond the fort the required path stays on the northern brow of the mountain and rounds a grassy hollow highlighted by an old miners' lake basking in its lower reaches. On the far side of the hollow, a narrow path takes you down towards the lake. This fades as it approaches the trees shrouding the near side of the lake, but turn right by those trees to the lake's dam, and locate the path leading from the dam to the mine workings on your right.

7 The path passes though the area of spoil heaps to reach a grassy platform beneath quarried cliffs. Stay with the path to the top pulley house, which overlooks a series of grass tramways; these tramways will form the descent route. The lowest of the tramways is less well defined, and a grassy path threads through gorse as it reaches the field at the base of the hill. The route runs parallel to a road before going over a ladder stile on to it. Turn right along what used to be the coast road, but now just serves some factories.

8 Turn left along a busy road, which links the old road to the modern dual carriageway. Continue straight ahead, negotiating the crossings of the slip roads with care. At the T-junction beyond the dual carriageway, turn left passing a caravan site before reaching the beach. Now turn right on a path running alongside the sand dunes. At low tide you'll be able to switch to the beach, but at very high tides you'll need to follow the dune path by the golf course all the way to the Conwy

Marina. Llandudno, the Great Orme and the Conwy Estuary can be seen clearly ahead and the sea breezes make the walk quite exhilarating and a fitting finale after the mountain walking.

9 The coast path bends right into the Conwy Estuary and reaches a jetty. Turn right here, inland, passing through a car park to the Conwy Marina, where scores of luxury yachts are berthed. Follow the water's edge, before turning right by the Mulberry pub and its car park. Turn left along the road at the far end, then right at the junction to pass over the dual carriageway once again. The road, Morfa Drive, will lead you back to your outward route by the school. Turn left here and follow Marine Walk before retracing paths through Bodlonbeb Woods to the quay at Conwy.

Opposite: Conwy from Conwy Mountain.
Above: The shoreline beneath Conwy Mountain showing the tramway used on the descent.

Above: Taking lunch on the slopes of Foel-fras with Llyn Anafon below.

FOEL-FRAS AND NANT Y COED

The little Victorian seaside resort of Llanfairfechan lies in the shadow of the quarry-scarred Penmaen Mawr mountain, where the great Carneddau mountains drop to the sea. A short promenade is lined by Victorian houses overlooking a pebble beach.

A long narrow street tucks under the A55 expressway and the railway to link the coast with the main part of the village, which lies on the old coast road. To the south, narrow lanes twist through a vibrant community of shopkeepers and artists, past some picturesque cottages into the valley of Nant y Coed. A railway tourist poster described this valley as 'the loveliest sylvan rock and river scenery in Wales'. In the 1900s it was part of the Newry Estate owned by a Mr Massey, whose tenant John Rowland Jones would charge visitors for entry. In 1924 the local council purchased Nant y Coed and now maintain it for its visitors' enjoyment.

A little valley path starts this route to the mountains and is shaded by deciduous woodland of alder, ash, oak and sycamore. In spring bluebells and wild garlic proliferate, and look out for the star-like white blooms of wood anemone, also wood sorrel, a low creeping plant with delicate five-petalled white flowers tinged with lilac.

The northern Carneddau mountains provide a more sombre world, one where quarrelling ravens and buzzards replace the redstarts and pied flycatchers of the woodland. Highpoint of the day is Foel-fras, whose name means the prominent bare hill. This gently domed grassy giant, the most northerly of the Welsh three-thousand foot summits, has sparse crags but fine views of the entire North Wales and Wirral coastlines.

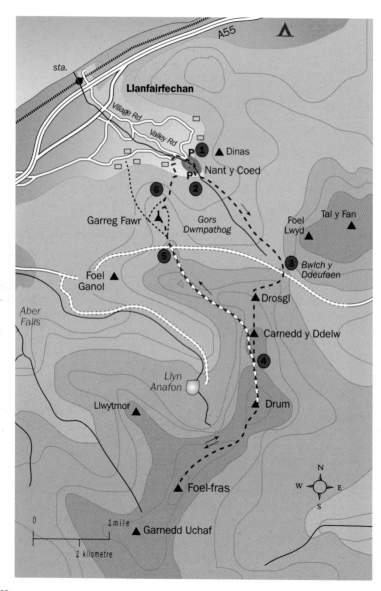

Distance 10½ miles / 17 km
Time 5–6 hours
Ascent 3085ft / 940m, moderate
Technical difficulty ••• (high mountain terrain)
Strenuousness ••••
Map OS Explorer OL17 Snowdon
Start / finish Small car park on Newry Drive, Nant y Coed, Llanfairfechan (GR SH 694739)
Public toilets At Llanfairfechan's promenade car park

1 Go through the gate beyond the car park and follow the stony path through the pleasant woods of Nant y Coed and by the north bank of the stream. The path passes a fishpond before descending to cross the stream using some substantial but smooth stepping-stones. More stepping-stones are used to cross a shallow side stream before the path climbs to a second car park.

2 A footpath signpost to the right of the car park points the way up the valley, and you cross a footbridge over the river to continue. Keep a sharp eye open for the concrete waymarking posts, which guide you along the zigzagging path in a complex series of criss-crossing tracks.

The path enters open moorland and starts as a grooved, rush-filled track. The concrete posts still persist for a while but where they point away from the wheel-tracks and downwards to the bottom of the valley ignore them. Stay with the wheel-tracks through an area of grassland and gorse bushes.

Gradually the route becomes less promi-

nent and grassy sheep trods continue through gorse fields, keeping an area of rushes well to the right. Aim for Bwlch y Ddeufaen, the col between Foel Lwyd and Drosgl, where lines of electricity pylons and a Roman road straddle the mountains.

3 The path arcs right just before the top of the pass and crosses the old road before tackling the steep grassy ridge of Drosgl. A ridge wall guides the route to the summit of Carnedd y Ddelw, where there's a Bronze Age cairn and a magnificent view of the Anafon valley and its small reservoir.

Above: On the stepping stones over the Afon Llanfairfechan in Nant y Coed.

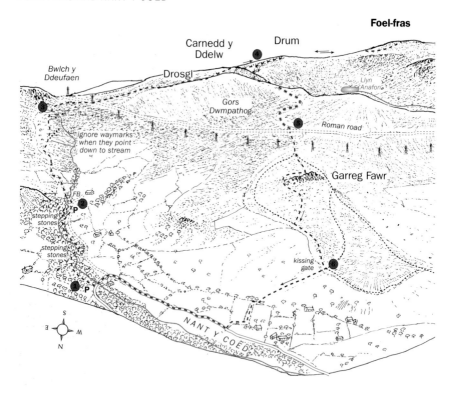

4 Beyond the cairned summit of Carnedd y Ddelw the path meets a stony vehicle track that has climbed up from Aber. This takes you easily to the summit of Drum. The route continues from the summit along the ridge to the boulder-strewn summit of Foel-fras. From here you can gaze southwards to the high three-thousand foot peaks dominated by the huge bulk of Carnedd Llewellyn, the highest in the range.

Return now to the summit of Drum, but on this return route stay with the stony track, which runs along the high sides of Cwm Anafon before switching to the north side of the ridge above the huge and desolate grass-and-rushy hollow of Gors Dwmpathog.

5 On reaching a crossroads of tracks go straight ahead along the one signposted to Llanfairfechan. North Wales Path waymarkers now highlight the route over Garreg Fawr. Stay with the track leading to the distinctive rocks which form the hill's northern summit. This is a delightful place, with fine views of the coast, including Anglesey and Penmaen-mawr Mountain, which looks down on the green pastures surrounding Nant y Coed and Llanfairfechan.

A danger sign tells you not to make a direct descent over the low cliffs beneath your feet. Instead, descend half-right (NNE) for a short way to reach a grassy track raking down left to the base of the cliffs. Now head north-eastwards to the substantial drystone wall running along the north-eastern rim of the hill. Follow the wall past the first ladder stile. A good path through more gorse bushes leads back to the North Wales Path, which comes in from the left.

6 Through a kissing gate, a splendid grassy terrace path lined by hawthorn trees descends the northern slopes towards the pastured valley of Nant y Coed. The scree slopes of Dinas (not named on OS maps) will be directly ahead. At the base of the path turn left though a gate and follow an enclosed path, which turns right. Beyond another gate turn half-left to cross a field diagonally to a laneside kissing gate.

Through the gate turn right along the lane, which descends to cross the Afon Llanfair-fechan, beyond which it reaches a junction with Newry Drive and Valley Road. Turn right again to return to the Nant y Coed car park.

Below: Descending back to Llanfairfechan (below left) from Garreg Fawr.

ABER FALLS AND MOEL WNION

Aber, more correctly known by its full name, Abergwyngregyn, 'the place at the estuary of white shells', is a small village on a grassy coastal plain at the mouth of the Afon Rhaeadr-fawr. The Romans settled in these parts and built a road from Canovium, their fort near Conwy, to nearby Gorddinag. On the east side of the village, tucked behind the cottages of the main street, is a grassy mound, all that remains of an eleventh-century motte and bailey castle. This was once home to Llewelyn the Great, Prince of Wales, who held court here in the thirteenth century. Llewelyn had placated his uneasy relationship with the English by marrying King John's daughter Joan, who would give him his heir, David. Unfortunately Joan had an adulterous affair with William de Breos the Younger, Lord of Brycheiniog. The prince had his wife imprisoned and de Breos hanged.

The Traeth Lafan (Lavan Sands) stretch for miles from the Conwy Bay coast at Aber to Anglesey, and have been designated a Site of Special Scientific Interest (SSSI). The sands and mudflats which appear at low tide are important for wintering birds, which include shelduck, teal and pintail. It is believed that before the encroach-ment of the sea this place was inhabited. A clue lies in its old name, Traeth Wylofain, 'the beach of weeping', which may refer to the sadness of those who were forced from their homes by the rising tides.

Until the construction of Thomas Telford's Menai Bridge in 1826, the sands were used by travellers crossing between the mainland at Aber to Anglesey, a distance of 4½ miles/7.25 km. At low tide they would trudge across the treacherous sands to a narrow channel, where a waiting boat would ferry them to the island at the Point near Beaumaris. In darkness or fog the bells of Aber Church guided incoming travellers.

The Coedydd Aber National Nature Reserve (NNR) is broad-leaved woodland with a wonderful diversity of habitats. The valley bottom is clad with oak, hazel, ash,

Opposite: the head of the glen with Aber Falls tumbling beneath the rocky cliffs and screes of Llwytmor Bach.

wych elm and alder set among areas of scrub, screes and grassland. In spring bluebells, wood sorrel and wood anemones proliferate here, creating glorious carpets of
flowers. In the swampier areas of alder the water-loving and fragrant meadowsweet
thrives. Up on the slopes you'll see rowan, hawthorn and crab apple, contorted and
warped by the wind. Lying at the valley head are the Aber Falls (Rhaeadr Fawr), one
of Wales's most unforgettable places, where a foaming river tumbles from its mountain habitat into the verdant and pastoral glen.

Below: Approaching Aber Falls.

Distance 7½ miles / 12 km
Time 5–6 hours
Ascent 2130ft / 650m, moderate
Technical difficulty ●●● (pathless sections near summit)
Strenuousness ●●●●
Map OS Explorer OL17 Snowdon
Start / finish Car park at entrance to Aber village (GR SH 655727)
Public toilets Forestry Commission car park above Bont Newydd

1 From the car park head back along the road towards the village before turning left along the signed enclosed footpath which passes a small information centre. Follow the succeeding lane through the village and past the Hen Felin (Old Mill) café, where they serve excellent food and refreshments should you have skipped breakfast. Continue past the last houses of the village to Bont Newydd, where the lane crosses the stream.

On the nearside of the bridge, take a gate to a path which heads upstream through woods before crossing a footbridge to the far bank, where you turn right on a wide path heading up the valley. Stay with the signed lower path to the falls, which passes to the right of the Nant Rhaeadr information centre. The falls appear ahead, first as a distant plume of white among the cliffs at the head of the valley. As you draw near their power becomes apparent as the torrential white waters thunder some 200ft/60m down the rocky cliffs into a deep pool below.

2 Cross the footbridge over the stream beneath the falls and head west on a path skirting the foot of wood-scattered cliffs before crossing beneath the slightly less spectacular falls of Rhaeadr-bach on a wooden footbridge.

3 On reaching the next stream, the Afon Gam, turn left over a ladder stile and follow a narrow path crossing the stream before climbing a spur of bracken and grass. The path is joined from the right by one that has traversed the mid slopes of Moel Wnion. Ignore the left turn, which fords the Gam beneath low gritty cliffs, but continue the climb on a path, which can be choked with bracken for about 20 yards/m in summer. It climbs a knuckled spur and soon becomes more obvious – you'll see the line of the continuing path ahead. Follow it over slopes to emerge on flatter terrain to the south of Moel Wnion. Ahead lies the bouldery little peak of Gyrn.

4 Turn right on a path to reach the saddle of land between the two peaks before climbing north on a narrow path to Moel Wnion's summit cairn, which has been hollowed out to form a wind shelter. Head north-east down from the summit to join a clear path running along the high sides of the mountain.

5 The narrow but clear path heads for the rocks of Cras. Don't be lured on to a narrow track descending left halfway along your path. The highest summit of Cras is a short detour to the left. There's a neat cairn topping the crags and fine views of the coastline, the great sands of Lavan and Anglesey.

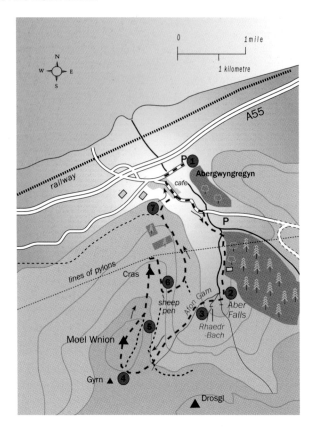

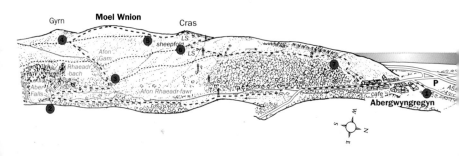

After returning to the main path, follow it north to a grassy hollow where three rows of electricity pylons cut across the mountains. Turn right here and follow a wide grassy path, which leads to a substantial drystone wall skirting the east side of the ridge. The path bends right to run alongside this.

6 On reaching a large sheepfold, cross the wall using either the ladder stile or a gate. The public footpath line marked on the map could be used but, after following a short grassy swathe through bracken to some thorn trees, it's easier to trend downhill with a fence to your right. You'll soon reach a fine grass track, part of the North Wales Path (NWP) route. Turn left along this, to pass beneath the pylons, and below a conifer plantation. Beyond a gate the NWP route turns left, but your route forks right to continue on the main track.

7 After 300 yards/m a waymarker highlights where your route leaves the track to the right. The path traverses hillsides of grass and bracken, with the village of Aber not far below. Go through the gate at the bottom of the hill and turn left on to the lane to pass through the village and back to the car.

Below: Climbing through the cwm of the Afon Gam below Moel Wnion.

TAL Y FAN AND ROWEN

History is very much the theme with this route, which climbs from the village of Rowen through pasture and woodland on to the rugged mountainsides of the Carneddau. The story spans from Neolithic times through the Roman and medieval eras to the present day.

Sheltered in a pastoral hollow high above the Conwy Valley and beneath the crags of Tal y Fan, Rowen is a peaceful village. Its name has several possible translations – *ro* means gravel or pebbles and *wen* can mean either white or holy. The Afon Roe flows by on its course from the slopes of Tal y Fan to the tidal Conwy. Its power was used by the three woollen mills which once stood here. Rowen was once much larger and boasted several inns, one of which, the Ty Gwyn, remains to this day. There are also a couple of fine country house hotels.

The last of the ancient Celtic tribes, the Ordovices, were farming on the high slopes when the Romans came. They watched as the invaders built their powerful forts and roads, and resisted them with all the resources they could muster. However, their situation was hopeless, and they were defeated by the irrepressible forces of Julius Agricola somewhere between AD75 and 77.

Tal y Fan, the highest point of the walk, means the 'end peak', and is the most northerly Welsh two-thousand foot peak. Topped by a stone-built trig point, its summit looks over a wide plateau which, like much of the Carneddau range, is scattered with ancient standing stones, hut circles and burial chambers. Lower down but still set in rugged mountain scenery between Rowen and Tal y Fan, the little church is dedicated to the seventh-century Celtic missionary, Celynin. It dates back to the twelfth century, although most of the current building dates from the fifteenth century. The gabled nave and chancel have roughly dressed stone walls and the seventeenth-century south porch is graced by a bellcote.

Opposite: Climbing the upper slopes of Tal y Fan with Foel Lwyd behind.

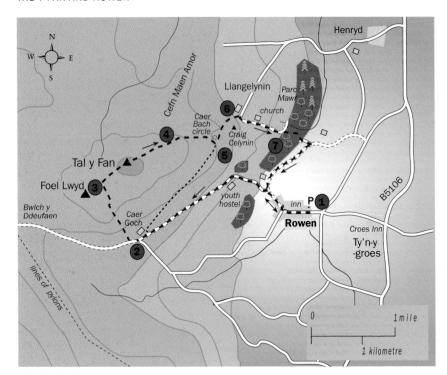

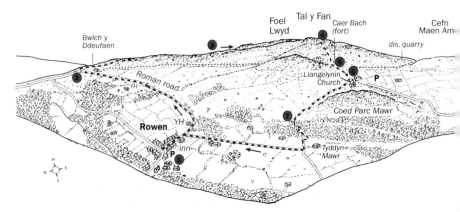

Distance 7 miles / 11 km
Time 4 hours
Ascent 2000ft / 610m, moderate
Technical difficulty ••
Strenuousness •••
Map OS Explorer OL17 Snowdon
Start / finish Rowen village car park to right off main road (signed WC/recycling centre) (GR SH 759720)
Public toilets Rowen village car park

① From the car park, walk back through the housing estate to the main road through the village, where you turn right. The narrow road accompanies the babbling Afon Roe for a while, then threads between charming cottages, an old chapel and the whitewashed Ty Gwyn Hotel, which is as fine a village inn as you'll come across in Snowdonia.

Turn right along the lane signposted to the youth hostel, and go straight on at the next junction. You're now in pleasant countryside with sheep and cows grazing in lush green pastures, and copses of deciduous woodland flanking the hillsides above. The cul-de-sac lane you're on has a sting in its tail, for its gradient steepens considerably beyond some woodland to the youth hostel at the top. Here the tarmac ends. A stony track, part of an old Roman highway between forts at Caerhun in the Conwy Valley and Segontium at Caernarfon, continues ahead, climbing more easily to the foot of Tal y Fan.

② After passing Cae Goch Farm the route briefly joins a tarred lane, which has climbed up from Llanbedr-y-cennin in the Conwy

Valley. After a few paces turn right to climb a ladder stile and continue along a narrow but clearly waymarked path, climbing the gorse-scattered lower slopes of the hill. Eventually it crosses a ladder stile in a wall on the right before climbing through heather and aiming for the gap between Foel Lwyd (left) and Tal y Fan (right).

③ On reaching the col, go over another ladder stile before turning right to climb by the wall up a steep rocky ridge to reach the trig point on Tal y Fan's summit. Beyond the main ridge a great barren plateau is laid out beneath you, stretching towards the blue waters of Conwy Bay, framed by the Great Orme and the Isle of Anglesey. The ridge walk continues north-east on undulating terrain with the wall still on your right. Occasionally the easiest ground is away from the wall.

④ Where the wall bends and descends half-right follow a sheep-trod of a path going straight on at first but then half-right parallel to, but well away from, the wall you've just left behind. The direction is east. The trod fades but soon a hollow of sheep-mown grass appears below you, flanked to the right by boulder and broken crags. Although pathless, your course descends easily to the intake wall above hillside pastureland. Immediately above it stands the old fort of Caer Bach (GR 744730). You should be able to make out a large ditch, the fort's northern ramparts, and a ring of stones encircling a large white boulder.

⑤ A grassy track now leads the route northwards with the rocky knoll of Craig

Above: St Celynin Church on the hillsides high above the Conwy Valley.
Opposite: Rowen village.

Celynin to the right. The track bends right, still beneath the knoll, and descends towards farm pastures. Beyond a large sheepfold it becomes enclosed by walls and bushes, and soon comes to the farm at Garnedd-wen.

6 Don't enter the farm complex but take a track on the right, which descends to pass to the right of the ancient church at Llangelynin. A gate in the wall allows entry into its grounds.

Beyond the church the track continues its descent across high pastures. Beyond a gate in a cross-wall the track descends towards the trees of Coed Parc Mawr to meet a wide track, which should be ignored.

7 A path continues the descent, winding through the beautiful woods, now managed by the Woodland Trust which felled the original conifers and planted oak and ash in their place. Interesting inhabitants of the woods are the lesser horseshoe bats, which have found favourable conditions in the workings of the old lead mines.

The track comes down to a lane just beyond a cottage, part of a scout camp. Follow the lane to a crossroads near Tyddyn-mawr farm. Turn right here. After about a mile, just beyond the plantation of Coed Mawr, turn left at a T-junction, where the outward route is met. The lane descends to the outlying houses of Rowen village. Turn left along the main street, passing – or maybe even stopping for refreshment at – the Ty Gwyn. There's also a good café on the right-hand side of the street.

Above: On the shores of Ffynnon Lloer looking up the crags to Bwlch yr Ole Wen.

THE HIGHEST CARNEDDAU

While in the north the Carneddau mountains are wilder and less frequented, to the south they are higher, grander, more rocky and 'real mountain'-shaped. Seven of the fifteen Welsh three-thousand foot peaks lie here, issuing mighty challenges to walkers and fell-runners alike.

Pen yr Ole Wen is the steep stairway to the Carneddau, especially the bold path behind the lake of Ffynnon Lloer. Fortunately there's an alternative and more attractive route using the mountain's east ridge. Once you've achieved Pen yr Ole Wen's summit, a delightful promenade on high ridges takes you to Carnedd Llewelyn, where you can cast your eyes across 90 per cent of Snowdonia, its mountains, its coastline, its estuaries and its islands.

Continuing along the high ridges you pass the climbers' grounds of Ysgolion Duon (the black ladders) and Llech Du (the black slab), but on the east side the path suddenly comes upon Craig yr Ysfa's amphitheatre, where great buttresses and gulleys plummet into the valley of Cwm Eigiau. On most days of the year the place reverberates to the sounds of climbers' voices and the clinking of their ironmongery.

Just beyond Ffynnon Llugwy Reservoir near the end of the mountain section of the route, you cross a concrete water-filled channel, which is part of a complex system of leats, pipelines and reservoirs scattered across the Carneddau mountains. These belong to the hydroelectric scheme originally devised to supply power to the aluminium works at Dolgarrog. It involved constructing a new storage reservoir, Llyn Eigiau, which was to be linked by tunnel to the enlarged Llyn Cowlyd. The consequences were disastrous.

On the evening of 3 November 1925 the Eigiau's dam, which had been built on unstable moraine debris, gave way under the pressure of the swollen waters. The horrendously powerful wall of water burst through the dam, wreaking havoc and flooding the wide upper valley of the Porth-llwyd before being channelled into the bottleneck of the Dolgarrog Gorge, high above the helpless village. Sixteen lives were lost that night.

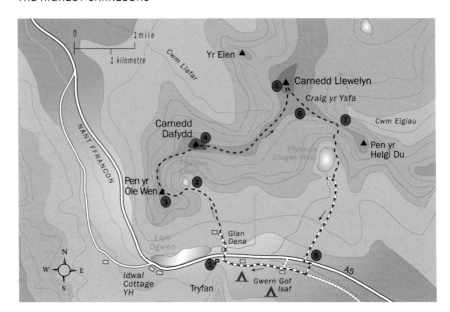

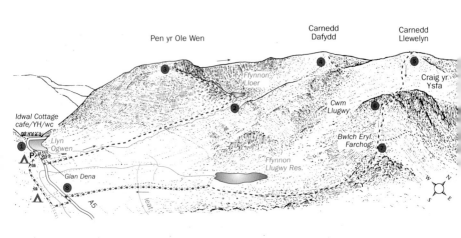

Distance 9½ miles / 15.4km
Time 5–6 hours
Ascent 3,575ft / 1,090m
Technical difficulty •••• short (but avoidable) easy scrambles on ascent and descent
Strenuousness ••••
Map OS Explorer OL17 Snowdon
Start / finish Roadside car park near Glan Dena at the east end of Llyn Ogwen (GR SH 669605)
Public toilets By Idwal Cottage youth hostel 1 mile / 1.6 km west along A5
Note In good conditions the 3,000ft ridges will be delightful; in bad visibility, navigation can be tricky

1 From the roadside parking on the A5 go down the drive past the conifers and the cottage of Glan Dena. Where the track turns left for Tal y Llyn Ogwen farm go straight on, following a wall north to a ladder stile. Beyond this a grass path, waymarked by the odd post, climbs steadily north over ground which can be marshy in places. After fording the Afon Lloer, it continues along the west bank to the shore of Ffynnon Lloer (moon lake). Its magnificent glacial corrie is overlooked by the rock slabs of Pen yr Ole Wen and Carnedd Dafydd's soaring slopes of grass and broken crags.

2 By looking left (south-west) beyond a marshy area, you'll be able to see your onward route – a boulder slope leading to the base of a huge crag at the foot of the East Ridge. Here a gully offers an easy scramble with good handholds. Above this a splendid path climbs the heather-and-crag spur rounding Cwm Lloer. The path divides short of Pen yr Ole Wen's summit, the right fork sticking closer to the edge – dangerous when there is snow and ice about. Pen yr Ole Wen's bouldery summit is extensive and has two cairns, one on the very top and one on the Ogwen edge.

3 From the summit the path dips gently to the shallow pass of Bwlch yr Ole Wen. From here you can look back down over the crags to the pear-shaped tarn of Ffynnon Lloer, now dominated by the sweeping scree slopes and broken rocks of Carnedd Dafydd's south flank.

A good path of boulder and grit, cairned in places, now climbs steadily north-east along the ridge to reach the cairn and wind-shelter on Carnedd Dafydd's boulder-strewn summit.

4 From Carnedd Dafydd's summit the path hugs the edge above the spectacular sun-starved Ysgolion Duon (black ladder) cliffs, which plunge hundreds of feet down to the stark, barren valley of Cwm Llafar. The cliffs are one of the main sites of the rare Snowdon lily.

Beyond the pass of Bwlch Cyfrwy-drum, the path begins to climb again on increasingly bouldery terrain. Carnedd Llewelyn gets bigger and more bulbous with every step – like an over-indulgent prop forward.

Carnedd Llewelyn's expansive summit is topped by a cairn and wind shelters but you'll have to go to the edges to peer into the surrounding cwms. Both Cwm Caseg (north-west) and Cwm Llyfnant (east) have small tarns in them. The former has another extremely charismatic peak, Yr Elen, soaring behind it in crag-capped scree slopes.

5 The continuing route heads ESE on a cairned path, which after a while leaves the crest of the ridge to skirt the high southern slopes of Penywaun-wen. The path regains the crest at the top of Craig yr Ysfa. Here spectacular pinnacled crags and a huge gully fall nearly a thousand feet into Cwm Eigiau.

6 A short craggy section beyond Craig yr Ysfa requires care, especially if wintry conditions prevail. The path descends further to the col, Bwlch Eryl Farchog, beyond which the whaleback of Pen yr Helgi Du blocks out all views to the east. Beneath and to your right is the reservoir of Ffynnon Llugwy. Its enclosing corrie is your way off the mountain.

7 At the col follow the path raking right, down slopes at the head of Cwm Llugwy. The path arcs to the left, and continues along the sides of Pen yr Helgi Du to join the reservoir's approach road. This descends to the A5 near Gwern Gof Isaf farm and campsite.

8 Turn left along the busy road, then, opposite the track from Tal-y-braich farms, turn along the track on the Glyder side of the road. Beyond some conifers and after crossing bridges over a minor stream and the Afon Llugwy, you come to a T-junction with a track running along the length of Nant y Benglog. Turn right along it to pass both Gwern Gof farms. To the left, the triangular rock wedge of Tryfan soars majestically into the sky.

The old highway returns to the A5 at the foot of Tryfan's great North Ridge. On the far side of the road is Glan Dena and the start of the walk.

Left: Looking down the Amphitheatre of Craig yr Ysfa. Opposite: Ffynnon Lloer from Pen yr Ole Wen.

CREIGIAU GLEISION AND LLYN CRAFNANT

The Afon Crafnant is the sweetest river, tumbling down from the fractured knobbly rocks of the Crimpiau–Craig Wen ridge, through a wooded rocky gorge to Trefriw and the wide pastures of the Conwy Valley. Crafnant means valley of garlic, and if you come in spring you'll smell the herb which still thrives in the woodland areas by the river. Near the head of the valley lies the near mile-long lake of the same name. This has formed behind a hard dolerite rock bar, which just couldn't be shifted by the glacier that shaped the glen. The lake was dammed in 1874 to provide the people with free water – and there's a granite monument at the north end of the lake to commemorate this. The area surrounding the lake was used for location shots for the 1981 film, *Dragonslayer*.

On hillsides to the east of the river you'll see many remnants of mines and quarries. The mudstones on that side provided good material while the old mill of the Klondike lead mine, although derelict, still looks imposing. The lead ores and waste have polluted the neighbouring lake of Geirionydd, so Crafnant is lucky they're out of harm's way.

The twin-topped Creigiau Gleision is an enthralling complex of rocky knolls, precipitous crag faces, heathery hollows and luxuriant beds of bilberries. The complexity and rich texture of the terrain contrast with the simple ridges and peaks of the higher central and southern Carneddau. The lack of wide eroded footpaths also adds to the experience.

Opposite: Llyn Crafnant at last light.

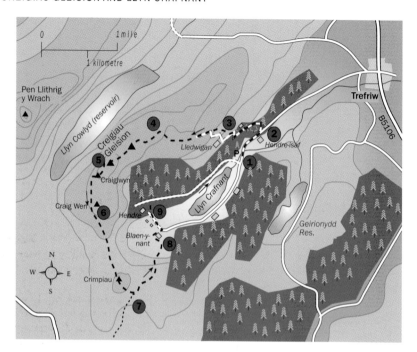

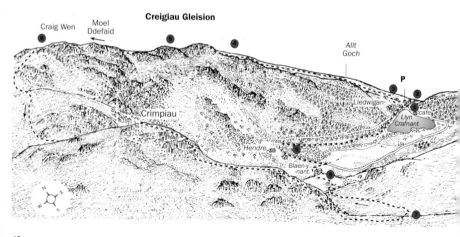

Creigiau Gleision

Distance 7¾ miles / 12.5km
Time 4½ hours
Ascent 3260ft / 995m
Technical difficulty ●●●, moderate
(navigation in mist would be challenging)
Strenuousness ●●●
Map OS Explorer OL17 Snowdon
Start / finish Forest car park and picnic site
(GR SH 757619)
Public toilets Car park at start of walk

1 From the forest car park turn left to walk back along the lane, which crosses the Afon Crafnant then runs parallel to it. You'll see the old slate mines of Hafod Arthen on the hillsides above the pretty woodland on the right.

2 About ½ mile/800m from the start of the walk you'll reach the first lane junction opposite the farmhouse of Hendre Isaf. Take the tarred left fork climbing uphill through woodland. Ignore the signed forestry track at the apex of a sharp bend and continue left along the lane to pass beneath a cottage. Beyond this the lane becomes stony.

3 The stone-built farmhouse of Lledwigan appears ahead but after a zig-zag you leave the lane for a waymarked path on the right. This winds up the hillside to reach a ladder stile. Over this keep straight ahead, ignoring a path doubling back to the right. The path becomes less distinct as it threads through scattered thorn trees, but waymarks highlight the route to another ladder stile in the intake wall. Now a sunken track climbs across rough moors of heather and moss.

4 The path reaches the ridge at a ladder stile near an intersection of fences. Beyond it a narrow path veers left through the heather. The ground steepens as the route turns right (west) with the fence before going over a ladder stile and turning south-west along the heathery ridge to Creigiau Gleision's lower north summit, which is topped by a small cairn. Some of the crags are streaked by gleaming white quartz. On the north-west side, precipitous heather-and-scree slopes with striated crags plummet to the shores of the Cowlyd Reservoir, which is over 200ft/ 60m deep.

A good path connects the north and south summits. The intervening heathery depression and rocky tors are typical of the whole of the ridge walk from here to Crimpiau.

5 From Gleision's main summit, the continuing path scrambles steeply down the south-west flanks to reach a clear path along a grassy section of ridge. The undulating path climbs to the summit of Craiglwyn, then continues across marshy ground before climbing over the shoulder of Moel Ddefaid. From here the path descends right to reach a path which crosses more marshy ground to the right of fine, upthrusting, angular crags.

Now there's the rise towards Craig Wen. The path climbs through the heather over its right shoulder, bypassing the summit itself before making a descent to a crumbling stone wall which winds along the knobbly south ridge. Using convenient gaps, the path will cross this wall a few times on its way to Crimpiau.

Above: The view from Creigiau Gleision's south summit to Tryfan and Ogwen.

Llyn Crafnant. The views are supplemented by those of the eastern Glyderau and Tryfan.

From Crimpiau's summit devious meandering paths continue in sporting fashion down craggy hillslopes. You're aiming for a col beneath the partially afforested Clogwyn Manod, and it doesn't matter which of the many alternatives you choose.

7 At the col you meet an ancient route linking Capel Curig and Crafnant. Turn left through a gap in the ridge wall to start the descent into the latter valley by way of a rough stony path through a narrow gorge, which soon opens out to reveal Llyn Crafnant. The track turns grassy and meanders down in fine fashion towards the fields and the cottage of Blaen y nant at the valley head.

8 On nearing the cottage the track comes to a stile by a gateway in a drystone wall on the left. Go through the gateway and follow the path ahead to the cottage. Turn right along its drive to the road end and immediately turn left. Follow the road past a couple of whitewashed cottages and over a river bridge.

9 On reaching the gate by the cottage of Hendre, turn right over a footbridge then left to follow the path beneath the house and up wooded slopes to meet a stony track. Turn right along this. The track widens into a forest road as it continues through the conifer forest, with views of Llyn Crafnant on your right. At the far end of the lake the track meets the road. Turn left along this to reach the car park.

6 Go through the first wall gap following a grassy path, which rakes across the hillsides with the head of the wide marshy hollow of Cwm Llewesig on the right. Be careful not to be lured on to the narrow right-fork path but instead climb on grassy and stone paths to Crimpiau's fine summit, an all-too-brief journey with startling views across tremendous crags and occasional glimpses of

THE EASTERN GLYDER RIDGES

I descended a great steep into Glan Llugwy, a bottom watered by the Llugwy, fertile in grass and varied by small groves of young oaks . . . The small church of Capel Curig, and a few scattered houses give life to this dreary tract. Yr Wyddfa and all his sons, Crib Goch, Crib y Ddysgl, Lliwedd, Yr Aran and many others here burst at once into full view and make this the finest approach to our boasted Alps.

Thomas Pennant, *A Tour in Wales,* 1778

In Pennant's day the quarries and mines were working at full tilt. The dreary village was a place of hard toil: of quarry dust, heavy drinking in the inns, and church on a Sunday. The mountains were always there, a spectacular backdrop with the odd miners' track straddling their ridges, but it was in Victorian times that they took on greater importance. Pioneers of climbing began to see them in a new light and, as the quarries and mines were shutting down one by one, the inns became a meeting place for this new breed of tourist. Capel Curig became the Zermatt of Wales, and Snowdon its Matterhorn.

The Eastern Glyderau, which stretch beyond the car park at the rear of the Pinnacle Café and climbing shop complex, provide a fine introduction to the mountain world of high Snowdonia. Although never breaking the three-thousand foot mark, their fine crag-and-grass ridges take you almost, but not quite, to the great rock peaks of Tryfan and Glyder Fach; they treat you to splendid perches where you can spy Snowdon, or look across sparkling blue tarns and lakes and even as far as Conwy Bay.

Left: On the eastern Glyderau ridge approaching Gallt yr Ogof.

Distance 9 miles / 14.5km
Time 5½ hours
Ascent 2430ft / 740m
Technical difficulty •••
Strenuousness •••
Map OS Explorer OL17 Snowdon
Start / finish Car park at the back of Pinnacle Café, Capel Curig (GR SH 720582)
Public toilets Behind café

1 The walk starts on the northbound cart track at the back of the car park. Turn left by a ruinous outbuilding of Gelli Farm.

2 Just beyond this you'll see a narrow, grassy track forking right, which will start you off on the climb. The track passes just above the farmhouse and fades first to a stony path, then into the grass. The route is very sketchy for a while as you twist between rocky bluffs. By the time you make Cefn y Capel, a path of sorts has established itself, mostly on the southern side of the ridge but occasionally popping up to the top.

3 The cliffs of Gallt yr Ogof loom across a wide plateau. The path keeps to the south of the summit but it's only a matter of clambering up a few boulders to get there. Llyn

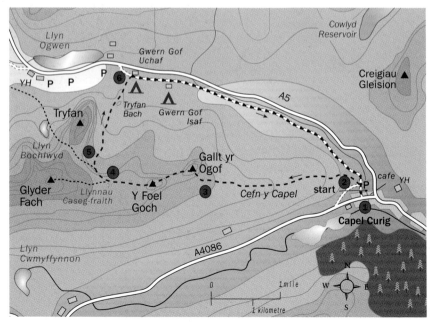

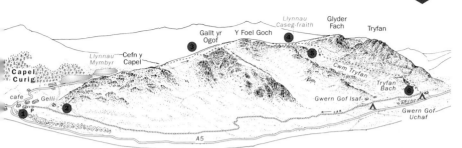

Cowlyd can now be seen squatting uneasily between Pen Llithrig y Wrach and the rock-and-heather peak, Creigiau Gleision.

Descend south-west along the craggy ridge to the grassy col, where you rejoin the main path. This veers to the right of a small pool and its marshy surrounds.

Again the path tries to lead you round a worthwhile summit but, as it approaches Y Foel Goch, just climb to the right to achieve the crags of the summit. The views of Tryfan and Glyder Fach are now tremendous, with the former's near vertical buttresses and cox-comb-shaped summit profile shown off to full advantage. Descend north to the grassy col south of the pools of Caseg-fraith.

4 Just beyond the last and largest of the pools turn off half-right on a path which rakes down the north side of the ridge. The bouldery path, part of an old miners' track, is heading for Bwlch Tryfan, but you should leave it for a path on the right, which will take you into the wild heather-and-boulder hollow of Cwm Tryfan.

5 The turn-off path is rough and steep at first, but the gradients soon ease. If it's a winter afternoon this part of the walk will be in eerie shade. But it's a rather magnificent eerie shade, with the now-black Tryfan reaching higher and higher into the sky as you descend among the heather and the boulders into the depths of the valley.

Near the bottom you are joined by the path off Tryfan's Heather Terrace and North Ridge next to a prominent tor, known for obvious reasons as Tryfan Bach (Little Tryfan). The last-mentioned is a popular place with climbers and there are paths to the right and the left of it. The two meet again at the far side, where you continue towards the farmhouse at Gwern Gof Uchaf. Over a stile you come to an unsurfaced lane. This was the main valley road before Telford's A5 was built lower in the valley.

6 Turn right along the track to go across the bridge spanning Nant Gwern y Gof and continue along a fine, fairly level track which makes a fitting end to the day, as you pass below the buttresses of Gallt yr Ogof. The cave referred to in its name (*ogof*) lies a quarter of the way up the crags to the left of a large gulley. After 3½ miles/5.5km, the track returns to the car park at Capel Curig.

TRYFAN BY HEATHER TERRACE AND LLYN BOCHLWYD

Rising from the shores of Llyn Ogwen like an almost two-dimensional wedge, Tryfan, 'the three tops', is no ordinary peak. It's as distinctive as the Matterhorn in the Alps or Suilven in the northern Highlands of Scotland.

The mountain was recently re-measured by independent surveyors John Barnard, Graham Jackson and Myrddyn Phillips, and many of its admirers feared that with its original height being only just above the three-thousand foot mark it might suffer the indignity of being declared below that magic height. Fortunately, the mountain was judged to be even higher, at 3010 ft/917.5m.

Tryfan's east face is its finest, with seemingly grassless precipices and buttresses rising from a deep heathery hollow. The west face is equally precipitous but more chaotic in its architecture. Its broken wall of crags include the famous Milestone Buttress, first scaled at the turn of the nineteenth century by climbing pioneer O. G. Jones.

Tryfan's steepness means there are only a few walkers' routes, and even these require the use of hands. However, the rock is generally stable with good handholds – and when you're on those slopes there's a surprising amount of vegetation.

Heather Terrace on Tryfan's east face is a clear diagonal shelf dividing the mountain's upper buttresses from its lower slopes. However, first-time visitors to the mountain will be surprised to find that it's nowhere near as obvious when seen close at hand, and many who look for the Terrace's lower end miss it and set off up the much harder North Ridge.

Opposite: Walkers tackling Tryfan's South Ridge.

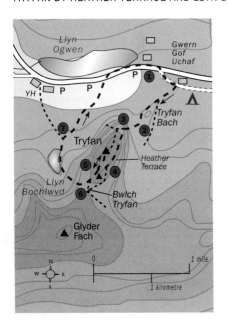

Distance 4 miles / 6.5km
Time 4 hours
Ascent 2065ft / 630m
Technical difficulty ••••• (some easy scrambling)
Strenuousness ••••• (steep ascent and descent of South Ridge)
Map OS Explorer OL17 Snowdon
Start / finish Lay-by car park east of Llyn Ogwen (GR SH 667605)
Public toilets Nearest either by Idwal Cottage youth hostel, Llyn Ogwen or behind Pinnacle Café in Capel Curig

1 From the A5 parking east of Llyn Ogwen walk eastwards for a short way before forking right on an unsurfaced lane, which takes you to the farm at Gwern Gof Uchaf. Go over a ladder stile to the right of the farmhouse and climb on a paved path towards Tryfan's great eastern buttresses. The path passes to the right of a prominent crag known as Tryfan Bach, popular with novice climbers. (There are paths either side of Tryfan Bach and you could use either.)

2 Beyond the climbers' slabs, the path veers right towards Tryfan. The steepening path passes through a little gully towards Tryfan's North Ridge but below the crest turn left towards Heather Terrace.

3 At the top of the gully but just before reaching the top keep a watch for a small path on the left – this is the beginning of Heather Terrace (don't go all the way to the crest of the path or you'll be on the much more serious scramble of the North Ridge.)

The route, mostly clear on the ground, is a mix of stony paths through the heather, bilberry and rock, and simple scrambles over low crags and outcrops. The dusky heather grounds of Cwm Tryfan and the old miners' track, which eventually leads to Snowdon's copper mines, are far below.

4 High up the terrace, the path divides. The left fork descends towards Bwlch Tryfan before climbing a scree path to the South

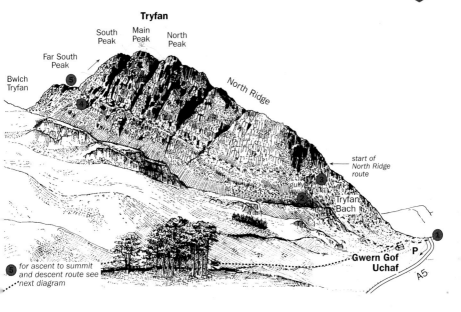

Tryfan

South Peak
Main Peak
North Peak

Far South Peak

Bwlch Tryfan

North Ridge

start of North Ridge route

gully

Tryfan Bach

Gwern Gof Uchaf

P

A5

for ascent to summit and descent route see next diagram

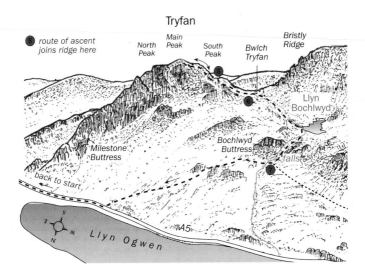

Tryfan

route of ascent joins ridge here

North Peak
Main Peak
South Peak
Bwlch Tryfan
Bristly Ridge

Llyn Bochlwyd

Milestone Buttress

Bochlwyd Buttress

falls

back to start

A5

Llyn Ogwen

Ridge. The right fork, an infinitely better course, sets off up a short scramble over boulders on the right, climbing towards the South Ridge. You'll see one of two ladder stiles on a grassy col ahead (between the Far South and South Peaks and marked on the OS map by the 850m spot height), but there's a steep drop over crags barring a direct route. Avoid this by continuing the scramble to the right and you'll come to the second stile, 20 yards/m to the right of the first.

5 Now the clamber up the South Ridge begins. Go over the stile. Straight up from the col is a steep rock step, but you can avoid this by taking a path which contours round to the left of it, then circling up to the right on a stony path between crags and boulders rising to a col between the South and Main summits. A short climb brings you to the Main Sum-mit, where you'll find walkers congregating around the monoliths known as Adam and Eve.

Return the way you came to the col between the Far South and South Peaks but this time don't cross the ladder stile in the wall. Instead, continue the descent on a stony path clambering down towards Bwlch Tryfan. The great rocks of Bristly Ridge dominate the view ahead towards Glyder Fach.

6 Just before reaching the col the path divides. Take the right fork, which arcs right on a clear descent towards Llyn Bochlwyd. The path, sometimes stony, sometimes paved, runs along the lake's eastern shoreline before crossing its outflow. Descend steeply on a clear stony path with waterfalls to the right.

7 At the bottom of the falls take a less well-defined right fork path, which re-crosses the stream above another waterfall and then descends north-east beneath the climbing slabs of Bochlwyd Buttress. The path becomes indistinct for a while as it crosses a marshy area, but once over a firm grassy knoll it re-establishes itself and becomes a pitched path descending to a ladder stile by a roadside car park. Cross the road and follow the pavement by Llyn Ogwen's shores and past the end of the lake.

Above: Llyn Bochlwyd and Y Garn seen from Tryfan's South Ridge.

Above: On Glyder Fawr's southern slopes with Snowdon's peaks on the skyline.

GLYDER FAWR AND GLYDER FACH
FROM PEN-Y-GWRYD

Built as a farmhouse in 1811, the Pen-y-Gwryd Hotel was soon turned into a combined farm and inn by local man John Roberts. In the mid nineteenth century a new owner, Henry Owen, considerably enlarged the building and changed it into a comfortable hotel. It became a popular base for climbers and in 1898 the Climbers Club first struck its roots here. By the 1950s the inn, now run by mountain enthusiast Chris Biggs, had become a centre for planning Alpine and Himalayan expeditions. Here John Hunt and his team, who in 1953 were the first to climb Everest, made their final preparations before departing for Nepal. The Climbers' Bar has a ceiling autographed by many world-famous names, including the summit pair Sir Edmund Hillary and Sherpa Tenzing Norgay, Sir John Hunt, Joe Brown and Sir Chris Bonington.

The hotel stands on the diamond-shaped site of a Roman marching camp on the road between Segontium (Caernarfon) and Chester, discovered in 1960 by Dr Josephine Flood. Today little more than mounds survive, and traces of a gateway on a crest just east of the Beddgelert road. The camp's northern ramparts are beneath the hotel, while the eastern ones are in the marshlands surrounding Llyn Lockwood, a trout lake constructed by the hotel owners of that name in the nineteenth century.

To save walking along the busy Llanberis road, this walk from the hotel takes an unusual pathless course beyond the camp to the summit of Moel Berfedd, a small mountain of moor grasses and rocky outcrops. Beyond Llyn Cwmffynnon you'll follow a path given many years before the CROW Act by landowner and conservationist Esmé Kirby, wife of Thomas Firbank who wrote the classic book *I Bought a Mountain* which, among other things, recorded the author's record-breaking Welsh Three-Thousands run of 1938. Esmé herself shattered the women's record that day by three hours, despite a ligament injury. The rest of the journey is a wondrous high-level walk over the rocky moonscapes of the plateau, past spiky rocks and along the fringes of rugged glacier-carved corries.

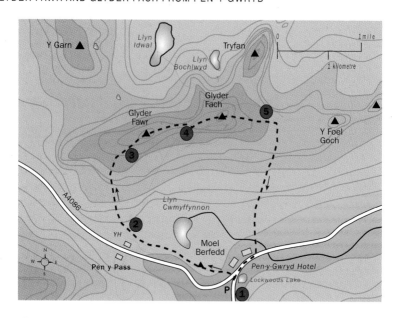

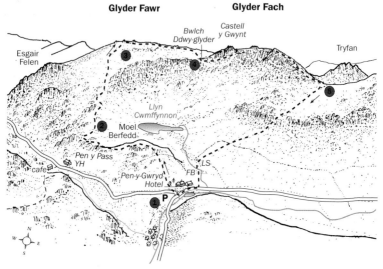

Distance 6 miles / 9.6km
Time 4–4½ hours
Ascent 2855ft / 870m
Technical difficulty •••• (some boulder hopping)
Strenuousness ••••
Map OS Explorer OL17 Snowdon
Start / finish Roadside car park at Pen-y-Gwryd (GR SH 660557)
Public toilets Nearest are by the café at Pen y Pass

1 The path begins from a ladder stile in the roadside fence left of the trees surrounding the Pen-y-Gwryd Hotel. Head west up grassland with the main fence to your left at first, then climb craggy slopes to the summit of Moel Berfedd. Descend the eastern slopes, now above the youth hostel and the café complex at Pen y Pass. The path from the hostel soon climbs to meet you and you continue straight ahead on a path up a long grassy arm, which forms a vague extension of Glyder Fawr's broad south ridge.

2 After descending slightly to a marshy area, the faint path climbs more steeply, north-west towards rockier ground. Occasional splashes of faded paint on the rocks mark the route, which climbs steeply away from the complex cliffs of the Llanberis Pass. The scene across the pass to Crib Goch and Carnedd Ugain is breathtaking, with views directly into Cwm Glas and the famous climbers' crags of Dinas Mot, Gyrn Las and Clogwyn y Person.

3 After weaving between rocky outcrops, the path veers right and comes to the edge of Glyder Fawr's stony plateau, where cairns lead to the main summit, a vast stony plateau scattered with scores of upthrusting crags and tors.

Follow a line of cairns across the plateau. These lead you to the northern edge where you first look down across Cwm Cneifion. The sharp ridge bounding this rugged declivity is Y Gribin, a favoured route out of Ogwen for scramblers. Beyond Y Gribin the ridge narrows and the path descends gradually towards Bwlch y Ddwy-Glyder, the pass between the big and small Glyder.

4 The way ahead from the col is blocked by the spiky rock tower of Castell y Gwynt – 'the castle of the winds'. A path descends to the right of the castle before clambering over the boulder slopes back to the Glyder Fach summit ridge beyond it. Although you'll lose a little height this way, it's much easier than scrambling up the rocks of the castle. The path continues across stony ground to the large pile of boulders marking Glyder Fach's summit.

Continue along the bouldery summit plateau past the Cantilever, a much-photographed gigantic horizontal slab of rock perched precariously on a couple of vertical outcrops. Just beyond this, on the northern edge of the plateau, the path nears the spiky top of Bristly Ridge, where excited scramblers will be stepping on to the plateau. Looking down you can see how the tremendously serrated ridge plummets down to Bwlch Tryfan, with Tryfan rising up behind as a steep-sided, stony pyramid. Now descend the bouldery east slopes of Glyder Fach, heading for the grassy col ahead.

5 Just before reaching the shallow pools of Llyn Caseg-fraith at the col take the right fork as the path divides. This is a shortcut to the Miners' Track, which cuts across the Glyder ridge on its way to the copper mines of Snowdon. On reaching this path, follow it across grassland to the southern edge of the ridge. Here the route descends the craggy upper southern slopes of Glyder Fach, passing the Nant Ddu (stream) beneath a fine cascade. Much of the rock is now interspersed with heather, whose summer blooms make a brilliant foreground to the wide southern vista, which includes Moel Siabod and the Moelwynion ridge, separated from the Snowdon Group by the verdant curving valley of the Gwynant.

As it nears the valley floor, the Miners' Track crosses then follows a drystone wall to the Nant Gwryd river, where a footbridge allows the route across an undulating field to meet the road just east of the Pen-y-Gwryd Hotel.

Right: Castell y Gwynt, Glyder Fach.

Y GARN AND THE NORTHERN GLYDERAU

In 1810 the renowned engineer Thomas Telford was commissioned to build a turn-pike mail coach road to Anglesey (the future A5), which included the now famous Menai Bridge over the Menai Straits, the channel between the island and the mainland. The existing road through the Nant Ffrancon, built by quarry magnate Lord Penrhyn, ran along the valley bottom, but Telford wanted to maintain a maximum gradient of 1 in 14 for the horse-drawn coaches, so at great expense he excavated the rock faces on the Carneddau slopes of the valley and built his road above huge stone ramparts. The project was completed in 1836 with toll houses placed every five miles – you can see the two nearest of these hexagonal buildings at Capel Curig and Bethesda. The famous outdoor centre of Ogwen Cottage was originally built as a coaching inn.

The route begins on the Cwm Idwal Nature Trail. Eighteenth-century writer Thomas Pennant came to Cwm Idwal and said it was 'a place to inspire murderous thoughts, environed with horrible precipices'. It was here that Idwal, son of Welsh prince Owain Gwynedd, was brutally murdered by Dunawd, to whose care he had been entrusted.

Cwm Idwal is a fine place to study geology and nature, and was declared a National Nature Reserve (NNR) in 1954. This perfect hanging valley was formed in the last Ice Age, when a small glacier slowly scoured and scraped its way over the cliffs at the head of the cwm, carving out this wondrous hollow before joining the huge glacier which filled the main valley of Nant Ffrancon.

Around Twll Du (the black declivity), also known as the Devil's Kitchen, is a deep defile where the mountainside's volcanic bedrock is divided by a column. At one time this was the snout of the glacier, and the base-rich soils on the surrounding ledges and crevices allowed many species of Arctic plants to flourish. The most famous is the rare Snowdon lily, discovered in the seventeeth century by Edward Llwyd. You

Opposite: Looking down Cwm Idwal from the Devil's Kitchen.

can see why it's called the Hanging Gardens as the foliage seems to flow down the rocks.

Above the Devil's Kitchen, the route tackles the northern Glyderau. Unlike Glyder Fawr and Glyder Fach, the ridges are largely grassy and provide splendid promenades on high tops, including one three-thousand footer, Y Garn. Although grass dominates throughout the long western valleys, the peaks rise out of Nant Ffrancon in splendid corries and ice-sculpted cliffs and spurs. This theme persists until the last footsteps back into Ogwen, where you can look back on those corries and cliffs from the valley.

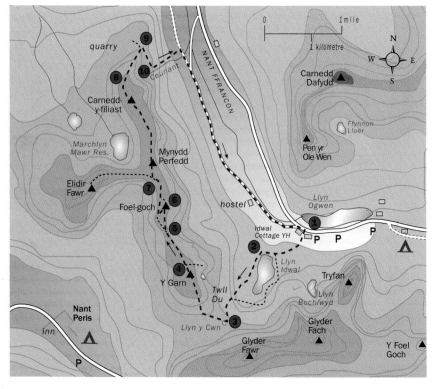

Distance 9¼ miles / 15km
Time 5½ hours
Ascent 3475ft / 1060m
Technical difficulty •••
Strenuousness ••••
Map OS Explorer OL17 Snowdon
Start / finish By Idwal Cottage Youth Hostel and café, Llyn Ogwen (GR SH 649603)
Public toilets By the café at the start

1 The bold Cwm Idwal path starts from the left side of the toilet block as a wide track, which climbs away from the buildings and past some boisterous waterfalls. The path swings right beyond a junction with the narrower Bochlwyd–Bwlch Tryfan path, to traverse open grassland with the great cliffs of Glyder Fawr ahead.

2 Soon the path arrives by the shores of Llyn Idwal. Turn right to follow the path around its north and west shores. Beyond the lake the path climbs to the foot of Twll Du, where it angles left on a high-stepped path up the rocky slope. The path emerges through a nick on the skyline and eases across slopes of rock and grass to reach the shores of Llyn Cwn (dog lake), which lies beneath the haphazard scree slopes which form Glyder Fawr's east face.

3 Turning your back to Glyder Fawr, climb the path north-west up the grassy slopes of Y Garn. The path divides: either fork will do, but if conditions are good, the right fork takes you to the cliff-edge much earlier than the left one. At the summit you'll get the best views of Cwm Clyd, which has two glacial tarns, one unnamed and the other called Llyn Clyd, bound by two rocky spurs.

4 From the summit the path descends on Y Garn's north-western slopes. Ignore the path descending right which would take you back down towards Cwm Idwal, but stay with the path down the stone and grass of the main Glyder ridge. Cwm Cywion soon comes into view on the right. It too has a small tarn in its seldom-visited depths. Ahead lies the next peak, Foel-goch.

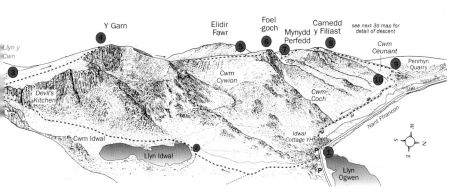

5 Take the right fork at the start of the climb as the left fork, the Welsh Three Thousands route, bypasses the peak altogether on its route to Elidir Fawr. The path you're on goes over a small grassy knoll before descending briefly to Bwlch y Cywion. From here, there's a short climb on grass to Foelgoch's summit. Divert to the eastern rim here to look down the immense cliffs of Creigiau Gleision. The cliffs continue beneath your feet and on Foel-goch's north-eastern ridge. Together they enclose Cwm Coch, the red corrie, where there's no lake but plenty of rugged atmosphere.

6 There are two choices now. The main path to Bwlch y Brecan zigzags down reddish screes and becomes increasingly loose – a horrible scar is developing. This could be avoided by backtracking towards Bwlch Cywion and descending right (pathless) on grass slopes to join the previously mentioned Welsh Three Thousands path. Turn right along this to meet the high path at the bottom of the scars.

The path continues to Bwlch y Brecan, where an old trade route crosses the ridge before arcing around the grass slopes overlooking Cwm Dudodyn, a long, wild and grassy valley stretching into Nant Peris.

7 Leave the Three Thousands path, which swings around left bound for Elidir Fawr, for the direct path to Mynydd Perfedd. This climbs steeply alongside a ridge fence to the mountain's south rim, where the fence turns left and ceases to be of any use. Maintain a northerly course over a stone-and-grass plateau to the cairned summit. The view by now is dominated by Elidir Fawr, whose angular outline and dark crags look magnificent as they overlook the man-made lake of Marchlyn Mawr, which feeds the Dinorwic Hydroelectric Power Station. The power station itself is built into the side of the mountain looking across Llyn Peris to Llanberis.

There's not much descent or ascent from Mynydd Perfedd to the next peak, Carnedd y Filiast, but the craggy scenery is stimulating. Looking back you can see Mynydd Perfedd has finer mountain form than you would have realised from its ridges, because the slopes are gracefully arced and ribbed with broken crags which accentuate the mountain's contours. Ahead of you here are Carnedd y Filiast's gigantic slabs, which rake down with unusual uniformity to Cwm Graianog. Carnedd y Filiast's summit is a jumble of large boulders and is topped by a windshelter.

8 After scrambling over the boulders of the south top for about 30 yards/m, the path rounds the rim of Cwm Ceunant before descending beneath the north top down the

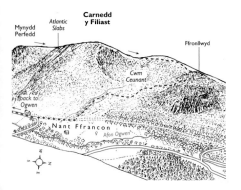

north-eastern ridge known as Fronllwyd. The narrow path winds down the ridge of heather, bilberry and crag, keeping well away from the ghastly Penrhyn Quarry. There's a short scramble down diagonal crags leading to a slight levelling of the ridge.

9 Not far below the crags you'll come to a small cairn, which marks the path shown on OS Explorer maps in black dashes. Turn right along this as it traverses the hillslopes of thick heather and bilberry on a course which is far more winding than the one shown on the map. Beyond the thickest of the heather the path curves to the left, and descends more grassy slopes before veering left again and coming to a prominent tree (GR 625637).

10 Beyond this and just short of the Ceunant stream, watch out for the path breaking left and roughly following the course of the stream downhill. Near the bottom of the slopes the path veers half-left away from the stream, crosses a streamlet and comes to a gate at GR 629639 by a stony track. Turn right along this to join a tarred lane, the old Bangor road, which takes the route beneath all the mountains you've climbed and back to the youth hostel and café at Ogwen.

Above: Foel-goch and Bwlch y Brecan.
Overleaf: The view of Tryfan and Ogwen from Y Garn.

MOEL EILIO AND THE ARDDU VALLEY

Llanberis was built out of slate, from the proceeds of slate, and is surrounded by slate hewn and exploded from its mountainsides. Lying by the twin lakes of Padarn and Peris, it takes its name from the Welsh St Peris who founded the church a couple of miles up the road at the original settlement of Nant Peris. Later the Welsh prince Llewelyn ap Ioworth (Llewelyn the Great) had Dolbadarn Castle built on a crag overlooking the village.

Quarrying at Dinorwig began in the 1780s to extract the Cambrian slates from Elidir Fawr above the shores of Llynnau Padarn and Peris. The quarries, owned by the Assherton Smiths, were never as productive as the Penrhyn quarries. Even so, after the building of a horse-drawn tramway to Port Dinorwic (Y Felinheli) in 1824 business boomed, with 3,000 men employed in supplying 100,000 tons of slate per year at its peak. The tramway was replaced in 1848 by the steam trains of the Padarn Railway.

After devastating the mountain into ugly terraces of slag, the quarry closed down in 1969 as slate was getting less profitable and operations were being hampered by collapsing spoil heaps. Part of the site has been taken up by the fascinating National Slate Museum and walkers also pass the old miners' hospital and the Anglesey Barracks. Part of the railway has been kept alive too, with little steam trains of the Llanberis Lake Railway chugging along the shores to and from Penllyn Station at the north-west end of Llyn Padarn.

Left: Moel Eilio with the Snowdon train in the foreground.

From the time you climb out of Llanberis into the Arddu Valley to the time you return to the village at the end of the day, you'll never be far from the sight and sound of the steam engines of another train line, the Snowdon Mountain Railway. The seeds of this idea came in Victorian times when railways brought tourists flocking to Wales, and a branch line from Caernarfon to Llanberis in 1869 took them on to the foot of Snowdon itself. Learning that the Swiss had successfully constructed rack railways up some of their peaks, Welsh engineers turned their attentions to Snowdon. Although the landowners, the Assherton Smiths, resisted for twenty years when they realised a rival scheme was being planned from Rhyd Ddu, they relented and in 1894 building work began.

After the engineering of the 5-mile/8-km route on the mountainside above the Arddu Valley, the Snowdon Mountain Railway opened on Easter Monday 1896. Triumph turned to tragedy on that first day when an out-of-control descending train derailed itself and hurtled down the mountainside. One passenger, Ellis Roberts, jumped from a falling carriage and was fatally injured. Thankfully, since that day the 2ft 7in gauge rack-and-pinion steam engines, with their red-and-cream carriages, have rattled and whistled their way up the mountain without serious incident.

Above: Llanberis seen from the lower regions of the descent route from Moel Eilio.

Distance 8 miles / 13km
Time 4½ hours
Ascent 2560ft / 780m
Technical difficulty •••
Strenuousness •••• (steep ascents)
Map OS Explorer OL17 Snowdon
Start / finish Car park on the shores of Llyn Padarn near the Electric Mountain Centre, Llanberis (GR SH 578605)
Public toilets In the ginnel between the car park and Llanberis main street

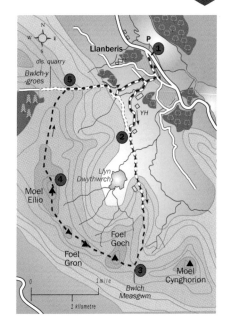

1 Go past the lakeside playground at the north-west end of the car park leaving it at the exit here. A narrow ginnel directly across the main road leads past the public toilets to the High Street. Turn left here before turning right up Capel Coch Road to pass the old chapel (Capel Coch). Go straight ahead at

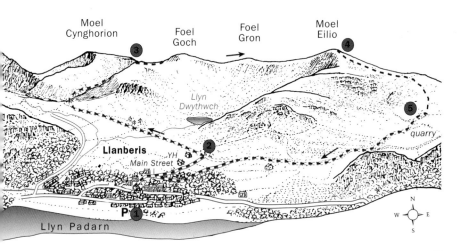

the next junction, where the road changes its name to Stryd Ceunant and climbs past the youth hostel on to rough-pastured hillsides.

2 Where the tarmac ends at the foot of Moel Eilio, turn left along the track heading into the expansive, wild valley of the Afon Arddu. On the grassy hillsides on the far side of the valley you'll see the trains of the Snowdon Mountain Railway, puffing up and down the line, their plumes of smoke billowing into the sky.

After skirting the base of Foel Goch's northern spur, Cefn Drum, the track swings right into the side valley of Maesgwm between the scree slopes of Foel Goch (right) and the crag-fringed Moel Cynghorion (left). It climbs to the craggy head of the cwm to reach a narrow pass, Bwlch Maesgwm, where you suddenly see the blue waters of Llyn Cwellyn and the granite dome of Mynydd Mawr beyond them. The shapely ridges to the west belong to the Eifionydd.

3 Go through the gate here before turning right on a steep climb up Foel Goch's grassy east ridge to the summit. The continuing ridge is a grassy rollercoaster with Foel Gron coming up next, then an unnamed peak (629m spot height). Various tight cwms give glimpses north-eastwards to Llyn Dwythwch, but it is the pallid scree slopes of Moel Eilio ahead which capture your attention as they get nearer.

4 A wide grassy breast leads to the rounded summit of Moel Eilio, the high point of the day. The retrospective views across the undulating ridges to Snowdon take on the appearance of waves on a green ocean.

There's a good path to ease you down the north ridge towards Bwlch-y-groes. Near the bottom take the less-defined right fork path, which cuts a corner to the quarry road and keeps well to the right of the spruce forest at the end of the high Waunfawr road.

5 Turn right along the quarry road, following it down westwards with Llanberis in the valley below and the quarry-ravaged 3000-footer Elidir Fawr rising behind Llyn Padarn. Just beyond the ruins of Maen-llwyd-isaf farm, the road meets the top end of a tarred lane. Follow the lane downhill, between farm pastures. On reaching the outskirts of Llanberis it turns right and meets the outward route by the chapel. Turn left and retrace your steps through the village.

Opposite: Snowdon at the head of Cwm Arddu as seen from the descent of Moel Eilio.

SNOWDON: THE CWM LLAN HORSESHOE

> For instantly a light upon the turf
> Fell like a flash, and lo! as I looked up,
> The Moon hung naked in a firmament
> Of azure without cloud, and at my feet
> Rested a silent sea of hoary mist.
> A hundred hills their dusky backs upheaved.
>
> William Wordsworth (1770–1850), *The Prelude*

Wordsworth and three companions set off from Beddgelert in late evening, planning to see the sunrise. After climbing through dense and damp hill fog, they arrived on the summit to see the moon lighting up a vast sea of cloud. In Book XIV of *The Prelude,* Wordsworth's imagination captured this sea as the world of the soul. The adventurous who bivouac on the top will know what he means but, if we daylight souls block out the sounds of the steam trains, the summit seagulls and the parties of excited schoolchildren, we may empathise with the poet as we survey the expansive mountainscapes and misty horizons.

Snowdon has five main peaks, Crib Goch (the red ridge), Carnedd Ugain (twenty cairns), Y Lliwedd, Yr Aran (the mountain) and the highest, Yr Wyddfa (the burial ground). The mountains have superb architecture formed by aeons of volcanic and glacial action. Ridges radiate in all directions, mostly rocky ones with great cliffs and gullies overlooking fine corries and tarns. Snowdon, as well as the highest, is also the most popular mountain in Wales, and boasts many routes to the top.

The Watkin Path used here was named after Sir Edward Watkin, a wealthy Victorian railway industrialist and Liberal MP, who built it as a donkey track, then handed it over to the nation when he retired. It was opened by Prime Minister William Gladstone in 1892, and this is commemorated by a plaque fixed on to what is now known as the Gladstone Rock.

Opposite: The waterfalls at Cwm Llan – an autumn scene.

The first recorded building on Snowdon was constructed by climbing guides in 1820, but by 1847 there were two competing hotels, the Roberts Hotel and the Cold Clubby, serving tourists who wanted to see the sunrise from the summit. In 1896 the Snowdon Mountain Railway bought both hotels and improved them considerably. However, by the 1930s the buildings were in need of repair and were demolished to make way for a new hotel designed by Sir Clough Williams-Ellis. It was built with large picture windows but these had to be made much smaller after they were blown in during a storm. Over the years, this building deteriorated and Prince Charles was moved to describe it as 'the highest slum in Wales'.

Its eventual demise came in 2006 and by 2009 a brand new café, Hafod Eryri, was built in its place, featuring non-reflective panoramic windows and sympathetic stone walls.

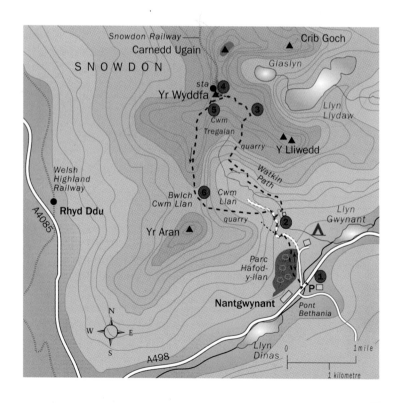

Distance 8 miles / 13km
Time 4½ hours
Ascent 3610ft / 1100m
Technical difficulty •••• (steep, friable path on final stages to summit)
Strenuousness •••••
Map OS Explorer OL17 Snowdon
Start / finish Nantgwynant Car Park (GR SH 628507)
Public toilets At the back of the car park

1 From the car park at Nantgwynant, cross the road and the bridge over the Afon Glaslyn before following a narrow lane opposite for a few paces. Turn left through a gate beyond which a delightful path leads through the woods of Parc Hafod-y-llan. The path meets a stony track, which leads out of the woods and winds over slopes of grass and bracken before passing to the left of some impressive waterfalls.

Beyond the falls the wide track cuts across an old quarry incline coming down from Yr

S N O W D O N

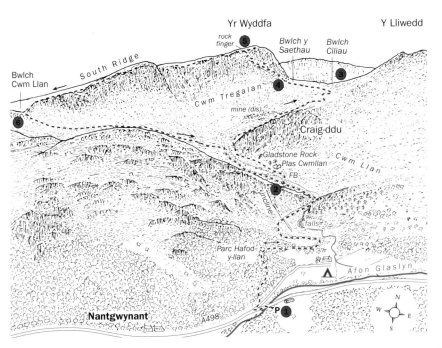

Aran's east ridge and continues by the river. The craggy hillslopes close in and the path climbs by the bustling river into Cwm Llan.

2 The Watkin Path leaves the old quarry track here and crosses a river bridge to the ruins of Plas Cwmlllan, once the residence of the quarry manager, but later laid to ruin after being subjected to target practice by soldiers in the Second World War.

Beyond the inscribed Gladstone Rock, the path swings left to round the precipices of Craig-ddu and some old quarry workings to enter Cwm Tregalan. This barren hollow is encircled by the crags of Snowdon's South Ridge, which culminates at the mighty Yr Wyddfa.

The path now swings right on the lower slopes of Y Lliwedd and eventually zigzags up to the ridge at Bwlch Ciliau. Now you look across the spectacular length of Cwm Dyli, with the majestic Yr Wyddfa cliffs looking across the tarn of Glaslyn and down the length of the much larger Llyn Llydaw.

3 Turn left along an almost level path to Bwlch y Saethau, where the paths divide.

4 Take the left fork, which rakes across loose rocky slopes to join the South Ridge halfway between Bwlch Main and the summit – the spot is marked by a finger of rock.

5 A short climb to the right leads to the summit where the modern glass-and-stone café of Hafod Eryri should be open to offer you well-earned sustenance. The view along Cwm Dyli is even more spectacular for you can see all of Y Lliwedd's thousand-foot cliffs and along the knife-edge of the Carnedd Ugain – Crib Goch ridge, including the pinnacles. The view northwards is dominated by the railway gradually descending the grassy escarpment to Llanberis. Wherever you look there are mountains of note in a view receding into the distant haze.

To go down, retrace your steps to the finger of rock high on the South Ridge. This time keep straight on down the South Ridge. This descent is dramatised by views to the left where the severe cliffs of Clogwyn Du plunge over 2000ft to Cwm Llan, a gigantic hollow enclosed by the stony flanks of Lliwedd to the north and Yr Aran to the south.

After a slight ascent to a subsidiary top known as The Saddle, the route heads towards Bwlch Cwm Llan (GR 605523).

6 At the pass, distinguished by a small tarn and quarry, the route descends eastwards on Yr Aran's grassy slopes to join the firm track of a dismantled tramway. Turn right along this to meet the Watkin Path and your outward route near to the stone ruins of Plas Cwmllan.

Opposite: Glaslyn and Llyn Llydaw from Yr Wydffa.

MYNYDD MAWR

Mynydd Mawr is one of the least climbed of Snowdonia's major peaks, partially because of the lack of footpaths. Seen from Waunfawr to the north the mountain appears as a great granite dome with a high rugged cwm (Cwm Du) ringed with broken crags. Venturing south through Betws Garmon, the crags of Castell Cidwm guard a secret cwm (Planwydd). But Mynydd Mawr's finest face is saved for the head of the Nantlle Valley. Here the pinnacled buttresses of Craig y Bera, popular with climbers and scramblers alike, are punctuated by scree gulleys.

Among the first things you'll notice are the sounds and sight of the steam railway running behind the Snowdon Ranger Youth Hostel (there's a request stop). The line has a chequered history of successes and failures. The original Welsh Highland Railway was formed in 1922 by the merger of the North Wales Narrow Gauge Railway and the Portmadoc, Beddgelert and South Snowdon Railway. The former ran from Dinas near Caernarfon to Llyn Cwellyn (Snowdon Ranger) in 1877 and on to Rhyd Ddu by 1881, while the latter had constructed a tramway between Portmadoc (now Porthmadog) and Beddgelert with a branch line from the quarries of Cwm Croesor. There were plans for a branch line from Beddgelert to the South Snowdon Quarry in Nant Gwynant but this was abandoned when the money ran out just before the First World War. In 1921 a Light Railway Order was processed to link the two railways, and by 1923 a continuous line ran from Dinas to Portmadoc. But it was not a success. In 1933 it went into receivership; the line was closed and the track ripped up in 1941.

In 1961 a group of volunteers started to restore the line, which became the Welsh Highland Heritage Railway (WHR), with a short line from the old British Rail sidings on the Porthmadog–Tremadog road to Pen y Mount 1½ miles/2.4 km north. Although initially against the WHR project, the newly re-formed Ffestiniog Railway decided to buy the track and started building back towards it from Caernarfon. The two ends were joined up in 2008 and a regular passenger through-service resumed in 2011.

Opposite: Mynydd Mawr reflected in Llyn Cwellyn's calm waters.

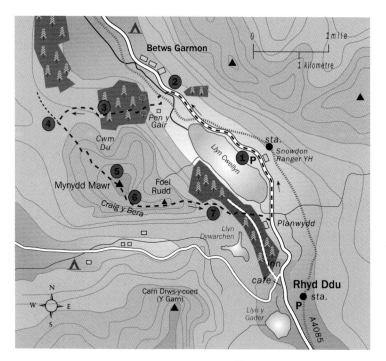

Distance 7 miles / 11 km
Time 4 hours
Ascent 2000ft / 630m, moderate
Technical difficulty ••• (could be difficult descending from summit in mist)
Strenuousness •••• (steep climbing in parts)
Map OS Explorer OL17 Snowdon
Start / finish Snowdon Ranger car park between Betws Garmon and Rhyd-Ddu (GR SH 563551)
Public toilets Rhyd Ddu Snowdon car park 1½ miles / 2.4 km south along Beddgelert road

1 From the Snowdon Ranger car park turn left along the road (in the Caernarfon direction) and follow it alongside Llyn Cwellyn's north-east shoreline.

2 On the approach to the first houses of Betws Garmon, the afforested hills squeeze in. Turn left along a signed stony track, which crosses a stone bridge over the waterfalls of the Afon Gwy, and the railway line, before turning left again to the cottage of Pen y Gaer.

Another footpath signpost points uphill towards the larchwoods of Tros-y-gol. The early and very attractive scenes are dominated by the rugged cone of Craig Cwmbychan and

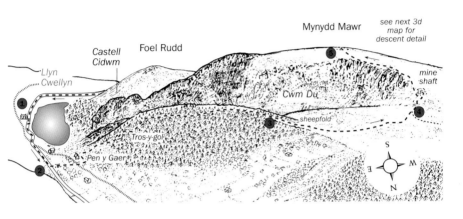

Mynydd Mawr

see next 3d map for descent detail

Foel Rudd

Castell Cidwm

Llyn Cwellyn

Cwm Du

mine shaft

sheepfold

Tros-y-gol

Pen y Gaer

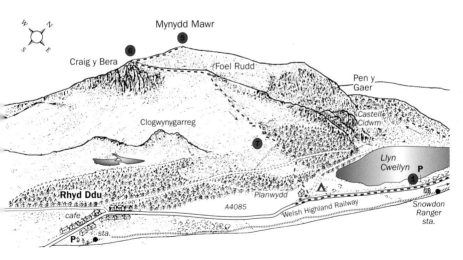

Mynydd Mawr

Craig y Bera

Foel Rudd

Pen y Gaer

Castell Cidwm

Clogwynygarreg

Llyn Cwellyn

P

Rhyd Ddu

cafe

sta.

P

Planwydd

A4085

Welsh Highland Railway

Snowdon Ranger sta.

Llyn Cwellyn beyond. Larch needles, tangled tree roots and slatey stones surface the path through the woods.

3 The path emerges at a step stile in the fence at the top edge of the woods, which are now dominated by pine and spruce. Ahead and left the rocks of Craig Cwm-bychan and the immense cliffs of Craig Cwm Du watch over a sombre cwm.

The path continues ahead (west) to some sheepfolds. Go over a ladder stile in a wall beyond them before angling right on a narrow path up heather slopes. This rejoins the wall higher up the hillside then comes to a marshy hollow. Keep a lookout for a narrow path on the left, which will take you up the lower slopes of Mynydd Mawr.

Although everything has been rural so far, across the heather slopes to the north and west you'll see the flanks of Moel Tryfan ravaged by quarrying and slate mining.

4 In turn the new path joins a wide path that arrives from the right and climbs to reach a fenced-off mineshaft, an outlier of the previously mentioned quarries and mines. The required path passes to the left and climbs along the clifftops of Craig Cwm Du before fading on the grass-and-moss slopes. Maintain a south-easterly direction to the mountain's summit, which is scattered with

boulders and has a few wind shelters, hollowed out from Iron Age burial cairns.

The view from Mynydd Mawr's summit takes in the coastline from the Llyn Peninsula and Anglesey right around to Caernarfon, where the castle stands out from the waters of the Menai Straits. Looking to the right you'll see the eastern face of Snowdon, the dusky corries of the Nantlle Ridge, and the angular outlines of Moel Hebog.

5 The onward route descends south-eastwards across the summit boulders to pick up the clear path along the rim of Cwm Planwydd, a corrie of scree, grass and heather and serenely curved slopes.

6 Soon the path arrives at the mountain's most spectacular spot – the top of Craig y Bera, where tremendous pinnacled buttresses cap scree slopes high above the Nantlle Valley.

The little path continues its downhill course, still on the rim of Cwm Planwydd, to Foel Rudd, which gives uninterrupted views of Llyn Cwellyn backed up by Snowdon. Now the path steepens and continues down a grassy spur. As it approaches the conifers of the Beddgelert Forest, the path zigzags to now-precipitous gradients.

7 The path now traces the top edge of the forest, then enters it by a ladder stile at Bwlch y Moch (pass of the pigs). The path descends through the trees to a flinted forest road. The path resumes on the far side and comes down to another track close to the farm and campsite at Planwydd. Turn right and follow the track out on to the road where you should turn left and follow the road (with care – it's busy) back to the Snowdon Ranger car park.

Note: Those who want to avoid the road at the end could turn right on the first forest road encountered on the descent. This leads to the B4418 Nantlle road just above Rhyd Ddu, where there is a café and an inn for refreshment. They could then use the Welsh Highland Railway to get back to the Snowdon Ranger.

Left: Nearing the summit of Mynydd Mawr with Caernarfon, the Menai Straits and Anglesey in the background.

CRAIG CWM SILYN AND CWM PENNANT

In the early stages of the walk you come across the largest of Cwm Pennant's slate quarries – named the Prince of Wales. If you look back down the valley you'll see a grass track winding into the distance. This is an old tramway which connected the quarry with Porthmadog, where the slate was conveyed to roof the rest of the world. The project was ambitious – at one time employing 200 men producing up to 5000 tons in one year – but its working life came to an abrupt end after only two decades.

As you continue over Mynydd Tal-y-mignedd down to the pass of Bwlch Drosbern, you see a change in the landscape. The narrow grassy interconnecting ridges of the northern end have gone, replaced by broad, boulder-strewn terrain. The change is due to volcanic activity and the rocks are rhyolitic ash flows known as the Llwyd Mawr ignimbrites. Llwyd Mawr, the line of crags just to the north of Craig-y-garn, was the centre of a great volcanic eruption, which produced a huge collapsed crater known as a caldera. The tuffs confined within this are around 700m thick, some of the deepest accumulations in the British Isles.

On the northern edge of Craig Cwm Silyn's summit, Craig yr Ogof and the Great Slab have provided climbers with excellent rock climbs, including some devised by pioneers such as John Menlove Edwards and Colin Kirkus.

The cliffs of Craig Cwm Silyn were also the scene of a tragic wartime air crash in 1942. Local quarrymen heard the drone of a low-flying aeroplane, then a horrendous explosion as it hit the

Opposite: Cwm Silyn and its lakes.
Above: The Cwm Ciprwth mine wheel.

cliffs. Rescue teams were unable to locate the RAF Hawker Henley and returned to the valley as darkness fell. The next day they found first the tailplane near the bottom of the Great Slab, then the fuselage wedged in a groove high on Craig yr Ogof. After clearing the wreck, the engine was rolled into the top lake where it still lies.

As the route descends past the wild heathery corrie of Cwm Ciprwth it comes upon a restored mine wheel by the stream. Copper mining has taken place in these parts since the Bronze Age but efforts were renewed during the Industrial Revolution. The copper mine here had two vertical shafts and a horizontal adit but was probably used as access for the mines of Gilfach further down the mountainside. The mines closed in 1894, victims of cheap imports from the Americas.

Distance 7½ miles / 12.2km
Time 5 hours
Ascent 2,855ft / 870m
Technical difficulty •••• (fairly difficult terrain in places)
Strenuousness ••••
Map OS Explorer 254 Lleyn Peninsula East or OL17 Snowdon
Start/ finish Car park at the end of the Cwm Pennant road (GR SH 540492)
Public toilets none

---

1 Beyond a step stile a clear path develops, highlighted by waymarking posts. It curves to the right and climbs the hillside towards some ruins, partially obscured by a large sycamore tree.

2 On reaching those ruins go over a ladder stile, climb a grassy bank and turn left over an area of slate waste. You're now on the course of an old tramway running the length of the valley but it doesn't manifest itself. A narrow path weaves between gorse bushes parallel to a slate fence. The tramway becomes clear again and continues towards the head of the valley. Beyond a boggy stretch it swings left, passes another ruin and heads towards the grassy slopes at the foot of Mynydd Tal-y-mignedd and the spiky arête of Craig Cwm Silyn. The view is dominated by a deep rocky gorge cut by the Ceunant yr Allt stream.

3 On nearing a drystone wall at the foot of Cwm Dwyfor the tramway turns right up an incline. At the top of this leave it for the start of the climb to Mynydd Tal-y-mignedd. The south-east ridge is ill defined at this stage and it is better to zigzag up the pathless grassy slopes. There's an old grassed-over wall that looks like a path but this isn't helpful – it's too steep. Gradually a ridge route does become clear and a very narrow path develops, taking the route up it and on to the main Nantlle Ridge to the south of Mynydd Tal-y-mignedd's summit. Head north to the summit obelisk.

4 On reaching the summit you'll see the impressive chimney-like stone column which

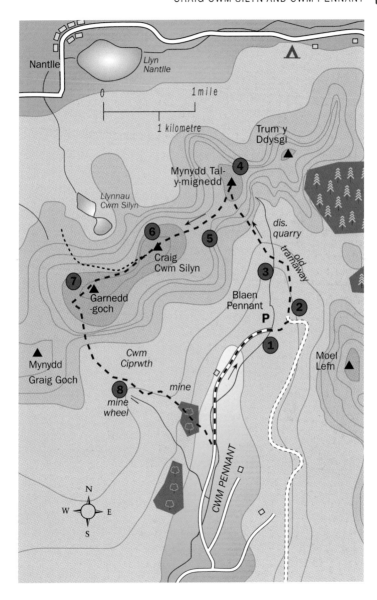

Nantlle

Llyn
Nantlle

0   1 mile

1 kilometre

Trum y
Ddysgl

4

Mynydd Tal-
y-mignedd

Llynnau
Cwm Silyn

6   **5**

dis.
quarry

Craig
Cwm Silyn

3

old tramway

7

Garnedd
-goch

Blaen
Pennant

P

2

Mynydd
Graig Goch

Cwm
Ciprwth

1

Moel
Lefn

8

mine

mine
wheel

CWM PENNANT

N
W   E
S

was erected to celebrate Queen Victoria's Jubilee. It lies to the right by the side of the wall overlooking the mountain's long north-west ridge.

We now retrace our steps across the gentle summit plateau. The path beyond heads for Craig Cwm Silyn along a grassy ridge descending gently SSW then more steeply WSW to reach the deep pass of Bwlch Drosbern. Although an old traders' track used to cross the ridge here, traces of it are hard to find today.

5 The rocky arête above Craig Pennant towers above you now with crags and screes making progress look difficult. The lower crags barring the direct ascent could be tackled head-on in an entertaining scramble, but most walkers opt for the easier path, which angles right to skirt the steepest crags before continuing on the boulders and grass of a broad ridge. Its steepness eases and gives way to a rough, bouldery summit plateau, where a cairned route leads to Craig Cwm Silyn's wind shelter and summit cairn.

6 The rough, bouldery terrain persists as you head south-west over two subsidiary tops, but after the second one grass takes over. Beyond a step stile in a fence head for the north-western edge to see the great crags and buttresses of Cwm Silyn. The three lakes of the cwm below are framed to perfection by the crags.

Ignore the path descending the rim of the cwm but instead climb back to the ridge wall. In the distance beyond a very shallow depression lies Garnedd-goch (the red cairns) topped by a stone 'man'. The terrain becomes bouldery again. Beyond a stile in a cross-wall the route reaches the summit and the 'man' transforms back into a quite unremarkable summit cairn.

7 From Garnedd-goch, the descent alongside a drystone wall is steep and rough. After 500 yards/m, watch out for a gap in the wall. Here turn left using the footpath marked on the OS maps, occasional upright stones marking this old byway. It descends to a point just north-east of Bwlch Cwmdulyn's nick,

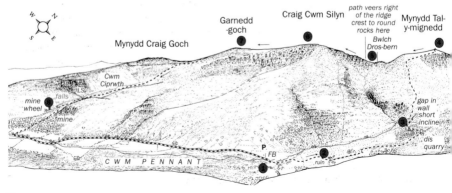

96

Above: Craig Cwm Silyn from Cwm Pennant near the start of the walk.

where another gap in a crumbling wall (approx. GR 510489) lets you through on to the Cwm Pennant side of the ridge. Paths have now disappeared and you're left to find the easiest course down into Cwm Ciprwth, which reveals its wilderness side, with dark heather and pallid moor grasses cloaking the shallow cwm.

The thickest of the heather hampers progress but by watching out for tracts of rough moor grass you can find easy ways into the depths of the cwm. Soon the route should take you near to the stream, which will guide you into the lower cwm. Eventually the stream cuts itself a rocky gorge and its flow becomes more boisterous. A ladder stile in a cross-wall (GR 521480) marks the start of a clearly defined waymarked path down grass and bracken.

8 The Cwm Ciprwth mine wheel comes into view and it's worth a short detour across the stream to take a look. The path seems unimpressed and stays on the stream's north banks, passing old mine workings before reaching the top edge of some beautiful oak woods. A stile lets you in and the descent continues in fine fashion, with the path still marked by yellow-arrow waymarkers.

Beyond a stile at the bottom edge of the woods the route crosses a field to a laneside gate at the valley bottom. Turn left here and follow the quiet lane up the valley back to the car park.

Above: Moel Siabod from the forest above Dolwyddelan.

MOEL SIABOD

As you walk out of the car park you can see that the Afon Llugwy is a powerful river. Its white-water torrents thrash heavily against the smoothed dark rocks. The old stone bridge, Pont Cyfyng, takes you safely across to the hamlet of the same name.

The ancient highway linking Capel Curig and Dolwyddelan is used to climb from the valley through woods and onwards to tussocky exposed moorland between the rivers Llugwy and Lledr. Later the wilderness views are tempered by spruce trees but the view of the crags and cliffs of Moel Siabod (pronounced 'moyle sharbod') does enough to keep things exciting. Soon you're through the forest and into a lake-filled corrie with the Daear Ddu spur to look forward to. It's a stairway of crags where you can scramble if you want to, or just weave between the crags, all the way to the rocky summit.

Siabod has one of the best views of Snowdon and its fine horseshoe walk, and these views extend to the Glyder and Carneddau ranges in the north and west, while the Rhinogydd, Cadair Idris and Moelwynion ranges fill those to the south and east.

Late on in the walk you come across the extensive whitewashed buildings of Plas y Brenin, which are beautifully situated by the shores of the twin Mymbyr lakes, from which you can spy the great peaks of Snowdon. Now the National Mountaineering Centre with a climbing wall, canoe centre, artificial ski slope and fitness room, the place was built in 1800 by quarry owner Lord Penrhyn as the Capel Curig Inn, providing luxury accommodation for wealthy tourists just off the 'Irish' turnpike and mail coach road (now the A5) which he commissioned Thomas Telford to build. The inn changed its name in 1870 to the Royal Hotel in recognition of its distinguished visitors, including Queen Victoria and later Edward VII, George V and Edward VIII. Its popularity and status as a stop on the 'Ancient Briton' Shrewsbury to Holyhead mail coach led to the expansion of Capel Curig. In 1955 it was renamed again, as Plas y Brenin, 'the king's hall', in memory of King George VI, whose trust fund had bought the building for use by the Central Council of Physical Recreation.

Near the end you'll see the Ty'n y Coed Hotel across the river and an old mail coach, the Yorkshire Rose, which lies beneath a wooden canopy. The 300-year-old inn used to be popular with slate quarrymen walking from Trefriw to the Siabod quarry high on the hillside to your left.

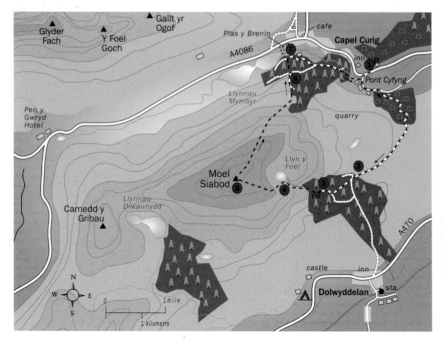

Distance 9¼ miles / 15km
Time 6 hours
Ascent 2560ft / 780m
Technical difficulty •••• (includes an easy scramble up the arête)
Strenuousness ••••
Map OS Explorer OL17 Snowdon and OL18 Harlech Porthmadog and Bala
Start / finish Bryn y Glo car park, Pont Cyfyng (GR SH 736571)
Public toilets Behind Pinnacle Café, Capel Curig junction

① From the car park turn right along the main road overlooking the bounding white waters of the Afon Llugwy. Turn left over the bridge, Pont Cyfyng, and follow the lane past the cottages, ignoring the main Moel Siabod

right turn near the start. After about ⅓ mile/ 500m, turn right along a stony track signed to Dolwyddelan. This passes behind the cottage and converted chapel, Capel Tan-y-garth. (This is the second converted chapel you'll pass. The road behind the first, a short way back, is marked private.)

This ancient highway of rough stone climbs through woodland, where moss cloaks the remains of old walls and rocks. The trees eventually thin out to reveal gaps of grassland clad with bracken. As height is gained the track continues across tussocky open moor, scattered with windswept gorse. It can get a bit muddy in the winter months but *terra firma* usually lies with its grass verges. Go straight ahead at the crossing of tracks and continue with moorland rising to sparse crags on the right, blocking out views of Siabod.

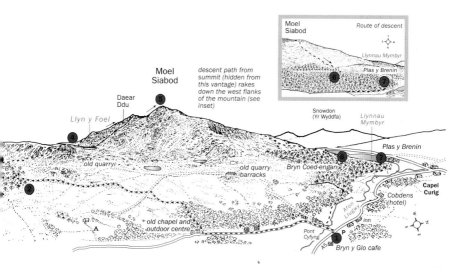

2 The track soon enters a large conifer plantation at a ladder stile. Ignore the track doubling back right on entering the forest but take the next right fork not far beyond it. You're now off the old Dolwyddelan road and heading south-west through the spruce and larch. Turn right at the next T-junction. The winding forest road you are on ends at a wooden footbridge.

3 Beyond this a narrow but clear stony path climbs over sinuous tree roots to a stile at the forest's edge. Now the narrow path climbs rough slopes of crag, heather and bracken. Threading through the craggy bluffs the little path comes to the dam of Llyn y Foel.

4 Turn left here, rounding the large corrie lake to reach the foot of Daear Ddu, a craggy spur rising to the summit. The ascent involves some easy scrambling, but unless wintry conditions prevail it's quite safe. For those who don't like too much excitement there's easier ground to the left of the crest. Either way you will reach the magnificent summit.

5 The way down starts unsurely. Ignore the rocky ridge top, but stay just to the left of it on the short grass. Eventually an increasingly bold path rakes NNE down the left side of the spur. The path becomes cairned and once over a ladder stile descends heather hillsides alongside the edge of a conifer forest with the white walls of Plas y Brenin prominent in the valley below. Eventually you enter the forestry plantations where a small stream to the left accompanies you further downhill.

6 On reaching a wide forestry track turn left, then leave it after a few paces for a path descending right and down towards the Mymbyr Lakes.

By the shoreline turn right along a forest track, which at first runs along the northern perimeter of the woods of Coed Bryn-engan. After passing the refurbished farm of Bryn-engan, now part of Plas y Brenin, take the less defined right fork track. This degenerates into a path, which undulates through the trees and around rocky outcrops to reach the Afon Llugwy near a footbridge – do not cross the bridge as this would take you back to the road at the Cobdens Hotel. The path you want now follows the river bank – take care as there are one or two points where the river has reclaimed the route making short diversions necessary. Soon the path leaves the woods and traverses riverside meadowland towards some houses. Beyond a footbridge over a side stream turn left along a track, which takes you to the lane at Pont Cyfyng. Turn left to cross the bridge then right along the main road back to the car park at Bryn y Glo, where there is a conveniently sited café.

Opposite: Climbing Moel Siabod's rocky arête.
Above: On the summit of Moel Siabod looking south across the Crimea Pass and the Moelwynion.

CNICHT AND THE NANTMOR VALLEY

Seen from the west Cnicht (the knight) rises from the pastures of Traeth Mawr and the woodlands of Garreg like a pyramid of solid rock. No wonder it has been called the Matterhorn of Wales. This bold facade is, however, just the front end of a long ridge which turns grassy as it melds into a complex of ill-defined ridges dotted with sparkling lakes and rocky tors. In the south-west Cnicht's sides are as impressive as its front, especially where crags and screes plummet into the cavernous Cwm Croesor. On this devious route we sneak up on the knight from the north, using a delectable streamside approach through the oakwoods and crags of Hafod y Llan.

In the summer of 1998 Hafod y Llan was put up for sale by landowner Richard Williams for £3.6 million. The estate, which includes half of Snowdon on the Nantgwynant side and Gelli-iago, where this walk begins, had SSSIs and listed monuments and buildings. Support quickly grew for the National Trust to purchase this special place and a public appeal was set up. International film star Sir Anthony Hopkins, who hails from Port Talbot, started with an amazing £1 million donation and Welsh rock group the Stereophonics chipped in with the £20,000 proceeds of a concert. In the end the appeal raised £5 million and the purchase went ahead.

Much of the land had been overgrazed by sheep and the natural vegetation and flora decimated. The Trust considerably reduced the 'woolly locusts' and at the same time re-introduced organically farmed Welsh Black cattle. Workers brought in to renovate the seventeenth-century cottage of Gelli-iago, unoccupied for fifty years, found over a hundred unpaired shoes buried beneath the fireplace. This puzzled historians but some believe it was an ancient ritual of concealment aimed at guarding a house against bad luck. The cottage lies next to the Nantmor Mountain Centre near the beginning of the walk. As you climb the winding stony path into a rocky tree-hung gorge above Gelli-iago and look across to a stunning Snowdon panorama, you may well feel that conservation is winning and the landscape is all the better for it.

Opposite: Cnicht's long summit ridge.

CNICHT AND THE NANTMOR VALLEY

The route finds an entertaining path up boulder slopes on the side of Cnicht before tackling the upper rocky cone high above Croesor. As you walk the ridge you may well come across the flowers of Grass of Parnassus, which thrives in the acidic soils of the ridge's marshy places, like those surrounding some of the lakes. The plant has heart-shaped leaves and solitary white flowers at the end of a longish stem. Many of the lakes are breeding grounds for the now not-so-common sandpiper, a small wading bird with sandy brown head and wings and a white throat.

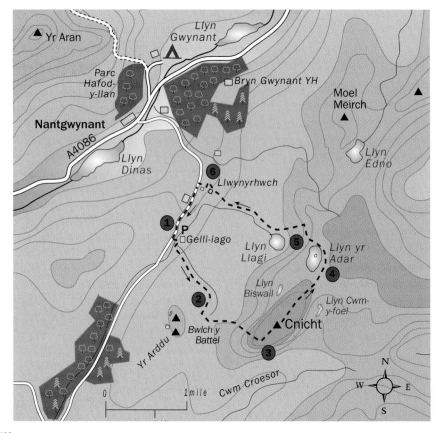

Distance 6½ miles / 11km
Time 5 hours
Ascent 2265ft / 690m
Technical difficulty •••• (short steep stretch to Cnicht's summit)
Strenuousness •••
Map OS Explorer OL17 Snowdon
Start / finish Car parking just north of Gelli-iago cottage (GR SH 633486)
Public toilets None en route (nearest at Watkin Path car park, Nantgwynant)

1 From the roadside car park turn left along the Nantmor Road, then left again along the track towards the Nantmor Mountain Centre. Go through the gate to pass to the right of the cottage before turning right beyond another gate on to a footbridge across the stream.

A winding stony path now climbs the hillside with the stream on the left tumbling and splashing over rocks studded with rowan, hawthorn and heather. As the path climbs higher past the crumbling ruins of old farmsteads, Cnicht's rocky sides appear across wet, straw-coloured moorland. It's a wild and dramatic scene as is the retrospective view, which features Snowdon rising above Nantgwynant's green fields and oakwoods like the colossus it surely is.

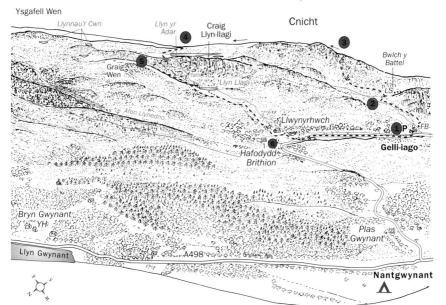

2 On reaching the pass of Bwlch y Battel the path comes to a ladder stile in a cross-wall. Beyond this you swing left beneath a crag-and-grass ridge towards a prominent scree run on Cnicht's flanks. A faint path develops and leads to the bottom of the scree. Now you scramble up the scree slopes to reach the crest path on Cnicht's south-west ridge.

3 Turn left along the crest path to scramble up the mountain's final rocky slopes. Although it's exhilarating, this route is never exposed.

Cnicht has two main summits and a third minor rocky knoll, but the one you're on now at the Croesor end is the highest. As you look along the undulating ridge the terrain changes to short grass and rock outcrops, a very agreeable place for a picnic. Looking westwards the long green valley of Cwm Croesor leads your attention to the glimmering waves of Tremadog Bay, which are framed by the Rhinogydd, the Eifionydd mountains and the Llŷn Peninsula. However, the most drama lies to the south, where cliffs and screes plummet a thousand feet into Cwm Croesor, and the gnarled crags of Moelwyn Mawr rear up in similar fashion on the far side.

When you've had your fill, head north-east along the ridge. Set in a shallow grassy hollow below to the left and surrounded by low craggy outcrops, Llyn y Biswail is particularly pleasing to the eye. The old quarry reservoir of Llyn Cwm-y-foel is shallower than it used to be. When full it used to look as though its dam was precariously sited on the edge of

the precipice and could easily give way and tumble into Cwm Croesor far below, but these days the water line has receded back into the lake's hollow.

The path continues along the ridge in a complex of rugged but ill-defined mountain slopes, which are capped by the low-slung peaks of Ysgafell Wen and Moel Druman. To the left now, in a wide marshy hollow, is Llyn yr Adar, a fairly large lake with an island in the centre. The continuing path will head in this direction.

4 The route leaves the ridge by a small cairn at the 631m spot height marked on the OS map. A faint path keeps to the driest ground, rounding Llyn yr Adar to the east and the north before heading north-westwards, past the outflow stream to the craggy edge to left of Y Cyrniau. It then descends northwards along a grassy rake beneath rock outcrops. To your left spectacular cliffs and a spout-like waterfall plummet into a near-circular tarn, Llyn Llagi.

5 After entering a V-shaped rocky hollow turn left along a good path descending west towards the marshy grounds at the foot of the lake. Always highlighted by the views to Snowdon, the path continues its descent to the right of the lake's outflow stream, threading between low rock outcrops and sometimes aided by stepping stones over the wet bits.

The path comes to a ladder stile at the top edge of some oakwoods and crags. The path beyond it comes down between the crags and beneath the trees to a field.

6 Turn half-left towards the whitewashed farmhouse of Llwynyrhwch, then left to pass in front of it. Over another stile in a wall the path turns half-right, heading towards another cottage, which it passes after crossing a bridge over a stream. Where the cottage's approach track turns left climb on the path straight ahead. This rejoins the track as it ends on the Nantmor lane.

Turn left along the lane, past the converted chapel at Blaen Nant and back to the car park.

Above: Above Gelli-iago with Snowdon in the background.

ABERGLASLYN AND MYNYDD SYGUN

Beddgelert's sandy-coloured stone cottages, shops, cafés and inns all huddle around a picturesque twin-arched stone bridge near the confluence of the Glaslyn and Colwyn valleys. It's surrounded by the lusciously wooded lower crags and bluffs of Snowdon, scenes that once made it to Hollywood – the Ingrid Bergman film *The Inn of the Sixth Happiness* was shot here.

Beddgelert, which means Celert's grave, takes its name from the Celtic St Celert, who founded the original church here. The current St Mary's Parish Church dates back to the twelfth century. An Augustinian priory was established in the thirteenth century and gained influence through the support of Welsh nobles including Llewelyn the Great. It is likely that Henry VIII had the priory dismantled, leaving only the chapel standing.

Above: Beddgelert.

Mynydd Sygun towers above the village with its bold craggy slopes cloaked with many thousands of rhododendron bushes. It's a pretty site for one month in early summer, but is considered a blight to the landscape by naturalists as this alien species chokes all other life beneath its canopy. Soon you rise above such controversies and can walk free on the heather-clad rocky knolls of a ridge.

To the east of Mynydd Sygun in the high hollow of Cwm Bychan rusting gantries and spoil heaps remain from nineteenth-century copper mines. The cableway transported the ore down the valley of your descent to a crushing mill at Nantmor village.

Opposite: Aberglaslyn in bloom.

The excavations were short-lived, however, and the mining company, which had also boasted finds of silver and gold, ceased operations in 1875.

Eventually the route reaches Pont Aberglaslyn at the mouth of the Aberglaslyn Pass. Today you'll see the valley opens out to a wide, low plain of grassland but once this was under water, part of the Glaslyn Estuary. It was in 1811 that William Maddocks built The Cob, a huge embankment stretching all the way across Traeth Mawr, diverting the Glaslyn and reclaiming land for pasture.

Maddocks's grand plan included building an entire town, Tremadoc (now Tremadog), which was named after its founder, as well as a port, Port Dinllaen, to serve the main London to Dublin route. Unfortunately, Holyhead was chosen instead, and the last part of the scheme failed. Salvation came with the quarry owners, who built a railway across the Cob to access the new harbour at Portmadoc (now Porthmadog).

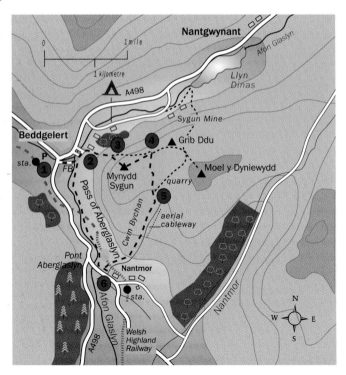

Distance 4 miles / 6.5 km
Time 2½–3 hours
Ascent 1345ft / 410m, moderate
Technical difficulty ••
Strenuousness ••
Map OS Explorer OL17 Snowdon
Start / finish Main car park, Beddgelert
(GR SH 588481)
Public toilets At car park; in centre of
Beddgelert near the main bridge

1 From the large village car park turn left, past the shops and cafés to the near side of the pretty two-arched stone bridge over the Colwyn river. Don't cross but go straight ahead on the narrow lane beyond the Tanronnen Inn and the craft shops, to cross the Afon Glaslyn on a tubular steel footbridge.

Again go straight on until you reach a fine terrace of cottages, where you turn right, then left along the lane at the far end.

2 After a few paces, turn right by a footpath sign to pass Penlan cottage, the former home of Alfred Bestall, illustrator of the *Rupert Bear* books. A rough, winding path beyond it tackles the steep slopes of rhododendrons.

3 Go through a metal kissing gate in a drystone wall, then take the right fork path climbing through more rhododendrons and heather to the cairn on Mynydd Sygun's summit. There are lovely views of Beddgelert's river valleys, with the powerful hulk of Moel Hebog stealing the limelight from the shapely Nantlle Ridge, which lies over its shoulder.

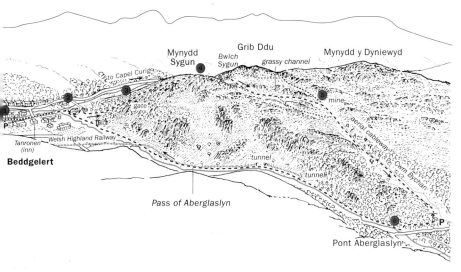

*Opposite: Climbing away from Beddgelert on the slopes of Mynydd Sygun.
Right: Grib Ddu from the Mynydd Sygun ridge.*

4 Now the route continues on a narrow heathery ridge towards the impressive twin knolls of Grib Ddu. Ignore paths to the left as you descend to the pass of Bwlch Sygun beneath those knolls, but take the one on the right which descends into a hollow of grass, bracken and heather, with a couple of shallow pools lying well to the left of the grassy path. The path weaves between rocky outcrops then enters Cwm Bychan, where it meets a wider path.

5 Turn right along this to pass the slag heaps and the remains of the aerial cableway of the old copper mines. The path follows the east bank of the stream at first but eventually crosses to the west bank before entering woodland. It passes under the Welsh Highland Railway bridge to reach a car park.

6 Now take a path on the right of the toilet block. This threads between trees and de-scends to the roadside by Pont Aberglaslyn. This stone road bridge spans the bounding white waters of the Glaslyn, which forge their way through a deep gorge lined by tree-hung cliffs on the right-hand side. The splendour of this scene can only be appreciated from a bridge-top vantage, so I would recommend you make the short detour.

The path wanted from here follows the boulder-strewn east bank of the river, way below those cliffs. On nearing the railway track the path gets a little bit tricky and has rope handholds to help you but any difficulties are short-lived and the path continues its course between the river and the stream, which is calming down by now.

Soon the railway crosses the path and the river while our route continues across pastureland. It reaches the edge of Beddgelert by the bridge of tubular steel crossed earlier in the day. Turn left over the bridge and retrace your steps back to the car park.

Above: Moel y Gest seen from the track used on the ascent.

MOEL Y GEST

The name Moel y Gest means 'bare hill of the paunch', a rather unkind description for although it is low by mountain standards it makes up for it with a distinctive outline and bold crags, which stand out for miles across Tremadog Bay and Traeth Mawr. Rearing up from the rooftops of Porthmadog, its dolerite rocks issue an irresistible challenge to visitors. Many crags have maritime names, such as Mainmast and Foremast Buttresses, and are popular with climbers.

This delightfully varied route begins at Borth y Gest, a quiet but beautiful backwater of Porthmadog set in a small circular bay. A rocky promontory separates the two places. Until the nineteenth century, Borth y Gest was a small shipbuilding centre for schooners used to transport slate from the local quarries. The clifftop houses at the mouth of the bay were known as pilots' houses, lookouts for those who found employment guiding ships into and out of the harbour. Here, too, was a crossing point between the Llyn Peninsula and Harlech, and locals earned money for guiding travellers across the treacherous sands and channels of the Glaslyn estuary.

The inhabitants of Borth could have done without William Maddocks: his Cob across Traeth Mawr, built in 1811, ended everything. Porthmadog grew from nothing to be the port of choice for the slate industry and the village had to content itself with being a small out-of-the-way resort for those wanting to take the sea air.

As you don your boots in the bayside car park and look across at the small craft bobbing on the harbour waters you may see oystercatchers, redshanks and Sandwich terns. If it's winter look out for goldeneye, great crested grebe and widgeon.

The coastal part of this route follows the Llyn Coastal Path through the Pen y Banc Local Nature Reserve. The mild climate provides an ideal environment for gorse, heather, blackthorn, oak and birch, which line the path. Again, it's good for birds and you might see curlew and pied flycatchers, maybe green woodpeckers if you're lucky. And when you've had your fill of the coast, the pleasing little inlets and the rock pools, turn your attentions to that peak. Get yourselves ready for an exhilarating climb, where you can if you wish get your hands on some rock.

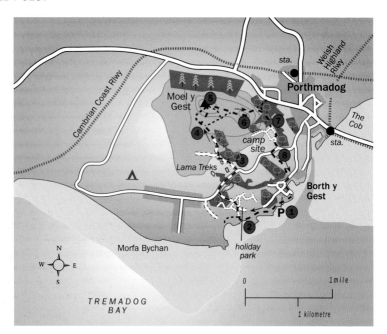

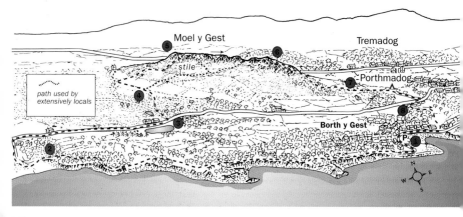

Distance 4¾ miles / 7.6 km
Time 2½–3 hours
Ascent 1200ft / 365m
Technical difficulty ●●●
Strenuousness ●●
Map OS Explorer OL18 Harlech, Porthmadog
Start / finish Car park at Borth y Gest
(GR SH 565375)
Public toilets At car park
Note When the rocks are wet they can be slippery and the route needs extreme care in snow or icy conditions

1 Turn left out of the car park along a short length of tarred lane, which leads out of the bay on to the headland where you enter the Pen y Banc nature reserve. A track above the rocks and sands is part of the Llyn Coastal Path. It takes you past cottages and weaves between thorn bushes and gorse. Frequent paths to the left will take you down to the inlets and the beach – not very useful if the tide is in, but if you fancy dipping your toes in the sea and taking to the sands there will be paths back to the coastal path. (The rocks of Garreg-goch are often surrounded by the tides and you may well have to come back to the coast path here.)

The main coastal path of wood palings and sand continues its course below the caravans and chalets of an extensive holiday park. But the views across the sandbars and waves of Traeth Bach compensate – if you look carefully across the sand dunes and marshes of Morfa Harlech you'll be able to pick out Harlech's iconic castle perched on its formidable crag.

2 At the far side of the holiday park, steps lead the path down to the beach at a pleasant bay by the manicured greens of Porthmadog Golf Club. Turn right here, inland, along an enclosed path beside a narrow lane. The path eventually joins the lane, which meets the Morfa Bychan Road. Turn right along this, using green verges for safety from the traffic.

3 After passing a lake and the woods of Parc y Borth on the right, leave the road for a left turn track through the double gates of the Black Rock Llama Treks – there is a footpath sign on the opposite side of the road. You may well see llamas beside the track.

Follow the track north-westwards to pass to the right of an anglers' pond. The track divides just beyond another gate and a ford. Take the lesser right fork track, which continues north-west through scrub and rough grasses.

4 Eventually you'll see pastureland to the right with the rugged flanks of Moel y Gest rising ever higher in the sky. Soon it is time to leave the footpath to tackle the craggy hill.

Option 1
The usual way, ingrained on the ground by the thousands of users of this route to access the hill, is to leave the public footpath track through a gateway at GR 548385. Although there seem to be no objections from landowners, the 100m across the first field is not a right of way – if you are challenged use Option 2 below.

After going through another gateway you're into access land and free to roam. The

Above: Borth y Gest.

clear path climbs the hillside towards a col between the east and west peaks. Half-way up the slope, watch out for a path on the left. This will take you directly towards the west peak; locate the stile in a cross-wall ahead. Beyond the stile the path rakes up to the left between the crags to join the ridge just short of the summit trig point.

Option 2

Continue along the public footpath track to the end of the enclosed pastures. Turn right on a narrow path beside the wall on the right, and then turn right along the top wall. There is thick bracken here but there are sheep-walks through it. Soon you'll see a tall metal gate in the wall. This marks the start of a narrow path, which weaves uphill through tall gorse bushes before following a wall on the right.

Just before a wall corner beneath Moel y Gest's upper crags, go over a primitive stile in the wall on your right. The path, now faint, angles up half-right then veers left. It reaches the ridge just east of the summit trig point.

As would be expected, the views are wide and the air bracing. To your right, beyond the houses and caravans of Morfa Bychan and the extensive Black Rock Sands, lie Criccieth's Castle and the town's wide sweeping bay. To the north the great climbing cliffs of Tremadog lead the eye to Moel Hebog, the Moelwynion where Cnicht shows its 'Matterhorn' western face, and Snowdon.

5 From Moel y Gest's trig point there are many little paths and most will offer you safe, if exciting, ways over this sporty crest. For those who find it too exciting, there is a path veering left just north of the crest on slopes of grass and bracken. This would lead you to the col between the west and east peaks.

For those who want to stick to the crest, head east, taking the left fork after a short way (the right fork was Option 1), then scramble over, up and down the rocks as they confront you.

Paths come in from left and right as you reach the col. Ahead is another easy scramble up to the east summit. The path down from here descends left just before the most easterly crag but it is well worth making a detour to the top for the bird's eye view of Porthmadog, its harbour and William Maddocks's famous causeway, the Cob.

6 The descent path weaves its way down more crags, with the highest ground to the right, before entering some oakwoods, where it comes to a junction. Turn right through meadows and thickets of bramble to reach a campsite.

7 Follow the campsite roads past the pub and the clubhouse and out on to the Morfa Bychan Road.

8 Turn right along this, then into a lay-by on the left. From here a footpath on the left passes through a little ginnel and past cottages before continuing across fields with the woods of Parc y Borth to the right. The path comes out on to Borth's promenade by the house of Borthwen at the north-east corner of the bay. Turn right and it's just a short walk past the café, the local shop and the Moorings Bistro to reach the car park.

Above: The ring cairn at Bryn Cader Faner.

BRYN CADER FANER

A winding road climbs from the coast at Llandecwyn between craggy hills to the little hamlet of Bryn Bwbach and one of Snowdonia's prettiest locations, Llyn Tecwyn Isaf. This lovely lake, fringed with water lilies and surrounded by oakwoods, looks upwards to the mountains of the northern Rhinogydd. The lake is full of carp, perch, rudd, tench and brown trout, while in summer watch out for dragonflies and damselflies. Raising your eyes to the hills, you'll see a bold rocky dome, Y Gyrn. Your walk will take you around the right side of this en route for the higher ridges.

The walk starts on a Bronze Age highway, later used by cattle drovers on their way between Talsarnau and Trawsfynydd. There are more relics of the Bronze Age on the low sides of the hill, including a burnt mound near Caerwych farm and hut circles, although these are not always clear to the untrained eye.

When you reach the high point of the day you're suddenly presented with the Bryn Cader Faner cairn, a Bronze Age burial and ritual site. Before the Second World War this finest of cairn circles, with a diameter of nearly 30ft/9m, had thirty stones looking in on a burial chamber. Unfortunately, soldiers, under a command unsympathetic to their heritage, used the monument for target practice. Although it's still very impressive – it's been compared to a crown of thorns – only half the stones remain upright. The position of the circle on a windswept shelf beneath the great cliff-ringed Foel Penolau and high above the waves of Tremadog Bay adds drama to the scene.

The onward route stays with the Bronze Age theme by following one of the ancient highways that linked Harlech and Trawsfynydd.

The route descends to the farmlands of Nant Pasgan where small enclosures of verdant pasture surround the listed medieval farmhouse of Nant Pasgan-mawr. This was the scene of a brutal robbery in which a wealthy drover, returning to Harlech with the proceeds of the cattle drove, was murdered for his monies.

Further down the hillside you'll pass a strange three-sided building just above the woodlands of Coed Caerwych. There are known to have been copper mines hereabouts and possibly this was a wheelhouse.

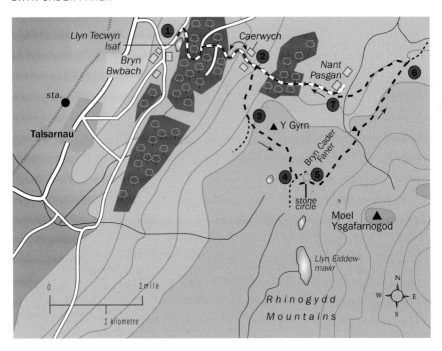

Distance 5¾ miles / 9.3km
Time 3½ hours
Ascent 1345ft / 410m
Technical difficulty •• (route-finding needs care in places)
Strenuousness ••
Map OS Explorer OL18 Harlech, Porthmadog
Start / finish Car parking by Llyn Tecwyn Isaf (GR SH 630371)
Public toilets None – nearest at Talsarnau

1 A narrow lane starts the route off around the north and east shores of the lake, then climbs through woodland and descends to a junction. Take the tarred road on the right then, at the next junction, go straight ahead through a gate signed Caerwych. The lane zigzags as it climbs through more woodland up to Caerwych farm and horse-riding centre.

2 Just beyond the house, and by the first of many Ardudwy Way signs, turn right to join a slightly sunken grass track, which passes through a gate at the far end of the pasture. Ardudwy Way signs continue to point the way uphill and into the access area just beyond

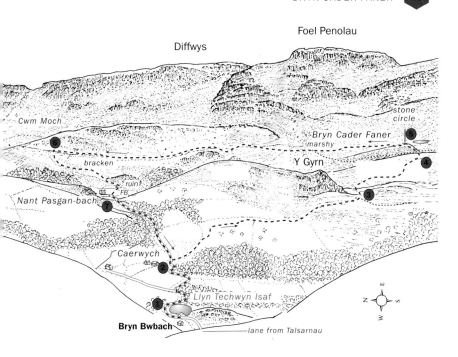

Foel Penolau

Diffwys

Cwm Moch

bracken

ruin

FB

Nant Pasgan-bach

Caerwych

stone circle

Bryn Cader Faner

marshy

Y Gyrn

Llyn Techwyn Isaf

Bryn Bwbach

lane from Talsarnau

the low rocks marking the Bronze Age burnt mound. The track continues beneath the western flank of Y Gyrn. Walkers will be spellbound by the superb views of the Llyn Peninsula stretching across Tremadog Bay. Behind this the celebrated Snowdonian peaks rise from the shores through Moel Hebog to Snowdon.

Take the signed left fork track. This hugs the south side of Y Gyrn, which now takes the appearance of a powerful, craggy tor. The track stays close to the foot of its southern crags, then crosses some marshy areas, using two footbridges to cross streams. Soon

the craggy peaks of the northern Rhinogydd's main ridge come into view.

After curving left around a marshy hollow the path joins the ancient track which crosses the range from Trawsfynydd to Harlech. On your right you should see a shallow pool set among rushes and marshy grassland, and ahead you'll see a narrow path climbing a low grassy ridge – this is the one leading the route to the stone cairn on Bryn Cader Faner. The little path arcs left along the low ridge and after a short way the cairn comes into view on the skyline. Its splayed-out stones give it the appearance of a crown, albeit a bit of an

unkempt one. You'll want time to take in the views, maritime ones in the west and of un-inhabited moorland topped by Rhinogydd crags and boulders in the east.

5 The map would suggest that you return to the ancient track I've just mentioned, but this would eventually involve what can be a difficult marsh and stream crossing. Instead, descend to the hollow on the south-east side of this low grassy ridge and turn left. Soon you'll come to an old track which heads north and meets the ancient track at the dry end of the marsh.

The old route is quite sketchy in places. Generally it heads north-east along a marshy shelf with the rocky main ridge high up to your right and the occasional rocky knoll separating one marsh from the next on the left. Beyond a very prominent sugar-loaf-shaped knoll, a wall comes in from the left. The path stays parallel to this wall, although it veers slightly right for a convenient stream crossing.

As the path climbs up slopes away from the stream it comes back to the wall at a narrow gateway. Don't go through it but continue along the wall's right side. Below you to the left now are the pastures of Nant Pasgan in which the austere medieval farm-houses of Nant Pasgan-mawr (right) and Nant Pasgan-bach (left) lie beneath squat rocky knolls.

6 Soon you come to another gateway and a junction of paths (if you overshoot this junction you'll be looking over Cwm Moch towards Diffwys and Craig y Gwynt.) Turn left through the gateway and follow an old miners' track raking down the hillside. After an area of bracken and beneath some small waterfalls the path comes to a ruined farm-stead. Turn right here across a primitive slab bridge, and head for Nant Pasgan-bach.

7 On reaching the house turn left down a cart track, which aims for the wooded gap between two hills. The track descends further to rejoin the outward route at Caerwych farm. Retrace your steps down the winding tarred lane to Llyn Tecwyn Isaf.

Opposite: Llyn Tecwyn Isaf at the start of the walk.
Above: Nant Pasgan-mawr with the backdrop of the Moelwynion peaks.

RHINOG FAWR, THE ROMAN STEPS AND GLOYWLYN

Known to geologists as the Harlech Dome, the mountains of the Rhinogydd are uncompromisingly rough. Consisting of thick beds of gritstone and shale formed in the Cambrian era over 500 million years ago – they're much older than Snowdon – the mountains in the northern part of the range display much-faulted rocks tangled with thick heather. These peaks don't have much in the way of walkers' ridges, for they are riven by deep transverse canyons, which go against the grain of the land. But these canyons provided convenient ways through the mountains for travellers.

In the west, approaches to the Rhinogydd take you through tremendous scenery. One such lane from Llanbedr follows the course of the frisky Afon Artro and its surrounding oakwoods before turning into Cwm Bychan at the head of the valley, where this walk begins. It's an enchanting place of contrasts. Green meadows and more oakwoods surround a fine lake behind which the crags of Carreg-y-saeth (rock of the arrows) soar without a hint of grass. The scene is mirrored on the north side of the cwm, where the equally impressive Clip buttresses look down on small enclosures.

The walk starts you off in the oakwoods and takes you to Gloywlyn, a rock-bound shallow tarn with rushy margins. Here no artist's hand could ever better the arrangement of the mottle of heather, bracken, moor grass and rock. Behind all this Rhinog Fawr, the objective of the day, awaits.

For all its rugged rock architecture, Rhinog Fawr has an aimiable summit, a smooth dome of heather and bilberry, scattered with boulders, especially around the trig point and wind shelter. The sea is always evident and it's near enough to the coast to get those salty breezes, but the finest view is of its neighbour, Rhinog Fach, a bulky hill of the usual Rhinogydd pattern of tiered crags and heather, this time backed up by Llyn Hywel, a fine glacial tarn perched high on its shoulder, and Y Llethr, the highest hill in the range.

Opposite: Above Gloywlyn on the slopes of Rhinog Fawr.

The descent takes you to another lake, Llyn Du, which lies beneath Rhinog Fawr's north face, before taking in the well-known Roman Steps, a paved staircase through Bwlch Tyddiad. Although Romans may have passed this way the steps are actually a medieval packhorse route used by cattle drovers. There's dramatic isolation at this place: a sense of sullen menace . . . could that be a highwayman on the rock above?

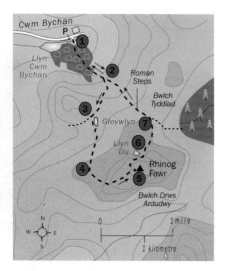

Distance 5 miles / 8km
Time 3½ hours
Ascent 2035ft / 620m
Technical difficulty ••• (route-finding needs care in places)
Strenuousness ••••
Map OS Explorer OL18 Harlech, Porthmadog
Start / finish Car park at Cwm Bychan (GR SH 646315)
Public toilets None

1 Go through the gate at the east side of the car park and turn right along a causeway over the three streams of the Afon Artro. Where the track starts to curve left go straight ahead on a path, which continues across fields with a drystone wall on the right.

After crossing a ladder stile, the path climbs under the canopy of oak woodland before re-emerging into a rugged valley of bracken and boulder. You are surrounded by typically Rhinogydd gritstone crags forming tiered and gnarled domes and canyons. The path crosses a fine one-arched stone packhorse bridge before continuing through an ever-narrowing cwm.

2 Most walkers are aiming to visit the Roman Steps but on this route you'll see them on the return journey, and therefore you'll need to watch out for the Gloywlyn path junction, which lies beyond a slab bridge and by a small cairn and gabion (a netted rock flood barrier).

The new path climbs to the right over a low craggy spur. Beyond this it threads through a bracken-filled hollow to another ladder stile at GR 649305 before following a narrow peaty path through more bracken. This soon steepens to climb rocky slopes interspersed with heather. Where the path divides take the right fork, which leads to Gloywlyn's northern

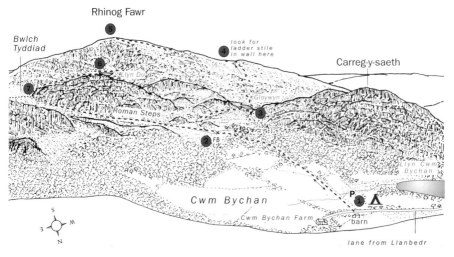

Rhinog Fawr

Bwlch Tyddiad

look for ladder stile in wall here

Carreg-y-saeth

Llyn Du

Gloywyn

Roman Steps

FB

Llyn Cwm Bychan

Cwm Bychan

Cwm Bychan Farm

barn

P

lane from Llanbedr

shore. The lake is beautifully sited, cradled by crags of heather and ribs of rock, with the craggy ramparts of Carreg-y-saeth (arrow rock) on the right side and the dome-shaped rock peak of Rhinog Fawr ahead.

3 A narrow peat path traces the lake's west shores. Be careful not to get lured on to a right fork path, which climbs over a low shoulder of Carreg-y-saeth before descending away from your objective.

Beyond the lake the little path climbs among rocks and goes over another ladder stile in a cross-wall to reach a heathery shoulder beneath the western flanks of Rhinog Fawr. There are scores of narrow trods through the thick heather and it saves time and effort choosing ones that get you nearer

Right: The Roman Steps.

131

to your objective, but eventually you'll be left to your own devices. Basically you need to climb south-eastwards to locate a ladder stile in a tall drystone wall at GR 652288.

4 Beyond this a well-defined stone-and-peat path climbs steadily if unspectacularly up the south-west ridge, passing a large cairn en route to the trig point on Rhinog Fawr's summit. There's a convenient wind shelter, should the elements be against you.

5 The route will now descend to the crag-bound lake of Llyn Du. It does this by following a path hugging the bouldery north side of Rhinog Fawr's west ridge. At a meeting of paths turn right, descending north-east to the top of a scree gully, which takes the route down to the lake shore.

6 Round the lake on its right-hand side. A narrow path continues and rounds the crags on the east side of the ridge, overlooking the conifers of Coed y Brenin (the king's forest).

7 The path veers left to enter the wild pass known as Bwlch Tyddiad. After squeezing through the barren rocky pass the route descends in a slabbed staircase. These are the so-called Roman Steps. Now you're walking through a canyon which wouldn't look out of place in a Western movie. One peak of layered crags on the right, Clogwyn Pot, looks like a cavalryman's drum.

The path meets the outward route by a cairn and slabbed bridge, and you trace earlier footsteps back down the valley, over the stone bridge and through the woods to Cwm Bychan's car park.

Above: Gloywlyn with Rhinog Fawr on the skyline.

Y LLETHR FROM NANTCOL

In the south the Rhinogydd mountains become smoother, less gnarled, with fewer ups and downs. The change begins on Y Llethr (the slope), whose craggy north face issues one last defiant stand before easing into a relaxing world of grass ridges.

This walk begins in Cwm Nantcol, a wide valley which weaves its way between rough pastured ridges before reaching the sea at Llanbedr. A twisting narrow lane gets you there and, after winding through woods and farms, leaves you in a pastoral arena surrounded by high mountains. Ahead are Rhinog Fawr and Rhinog Fach. The former peak's angular outlines display upthrusted gritstone strata accentuated by the darkness of its heathery hollows, while the latter's rugged crags and heather rise up in more haphazard fashion to an almost flat crest. Y Llethr is as yet rather undistinguished; its best features are hidden by the lower slopes of its western ridge.

Opposite: Diffwys seen across the Ysgethin valley from Y Llethr's west ridge.
Above: Walking into Bwlch Drws Ardudwy.

The route will follow an old drovers' road through Bwlch Drws Ardudwy (the door of the pass of Ardudwy), the ravine between the two Rhinog peaks. On your right is Maes-y-garnedd Farm, home to Col. John Jones around the time of the Civil War. While residents of the Harlech area were strong supporters of the Crown, Col. Jones had married Oliver Cromwell's sister and took an active part on the Parliamentary side, being one of the signatories of Charles I's death warrant. These deeds were remembered well by Charles II after the Restoration, and the new king condemned him to death. Diarist Samuel Pepys noted that the steaming remains of Jones's hung, drawn and quartered body were dragged around the streets of London.

The mountains close in and the skies recede as you enter through the door to the great Kingdom of Ardudwy, and the drama persists as you climb on to the lower slopes of Rhinog Fach and up to the gigantic Y Llethr slabs, which soar from the waters of Llyn Hywel. Now Y Llethr shows itself properly, a huge grassy dome ribbed heavily with rock strata, which arc gently down to the right. Y Llethr's summit is made from much younger shaley rocks, which overlie the Cambrian Grits, and so it is with Diffwys and the ridges declining south and west to Barmouth. Within this group of rocks manganese mines were developed, such as the Hafotty mines above Llanaber. The grassy rides of the southern Rhinogydd may not be as spectacular as the roller-coaster rocks of the north but they allow a free-striding return route into Nantcol.

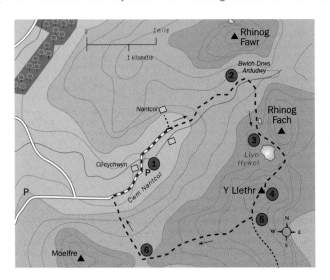

Distance 7 miles / 11.2km
Time 4½ hrs
Ascent 2065ft / 630m
Technical difficulty ••• (steep climb on
Y Llethr)
Strenuousness ••••
Map OS Explorer OL18 Harlech, Porthmadog
Start / finish Car park with permission (small
charge), Cil-cychwyn Farm (GR SH 634259)
Public toilets None

1 Follow the winding lane up the Nantcol
valley, through sparse pastures to the road-
end between the farms of Nantcol and Maes-
y-garnedd. A partially slabbed path continues
north-eastwards. On this you will climb ever
nearer to the narrow gap of Bwlch Drws
Ardudwy, where Rhinog Fawr and Rhinog
Fach close in.

In late summer the colourful pinks of the
abundant heather dispel the dark menace
of this place. The undulating path briefly descends to a wide marshy bowl. It traverses the
rushes of the hollow and stays closer to a wall
running along the length of the pass.

2 Turn right across the second of two
ladder stiles in the wall to reach a steep but
narrow path climbing through the heather
beneath the immense slopes of Rhinog Fach.
After a while you pass Llyn Cwmhosan, a
small tarn with a yellow rim of grasses, which
contrasts splendidly with the dark heather
and boulder of the mountainsides. When you
get just above this look back across the lake
and you'll get one of the finest views of
Rhinog Fawr and its angled gritstone slabs.

Ignore paths climbing left as they will
lead you on to Rhinog Fach. The main route
climbs further up a spur of rock and heather

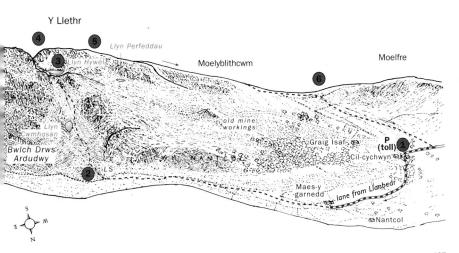

to come upon the shores of Llyn Hywel. Rhinog Fach now looks its Sunday best, a triangular summit of rock capping extensive screes flowing down to the bouldery shoreline of the lake. On the other side Y Llethr, your objective, looks more of a hulk, with its bold ribs of rock separated by grassy shelves and a little scree. Between the two are the Y Llethr Slabs, gigantic rocks upthrusted from the lake to the col on the skyline.

3 Cross the boulders on the north shore of Llyn Hywel to reach the top of the slabs at the col, and follow a wall to the foot of Y Llethr's crags. Now the path veers right, away from the wall. It becomes rough and winding as it tackles steep slopes up a grassy chute. The path arcs left and, as the breezes begin to waft over the skyline, you realise you've made it to the rim of the grassy summit.

4 Continue along the ridge southwards with the crag-ruffled Crib-y-rhiw leading your gaze towards Diffwys.

5 The ridge soon dives steeply, down to a ladder stile in a cross-wall. Here you leave the main Rhinog ridge for a rutted Land Rover track, which descends the west ridge. The track winds away from the wall for a while before rejoining it nearer to the col beneath the domed peak of Moelfre, which lies ahead.

The wall turns right and ceases to be any use but stay with the path until it begins to curve left down towards the Ysgethin valley.

6 Follow the crest until you see a faint path curving northwards to a gate in the wall along Moelfre's east ridge (GR 637248). (The bridleway on the OS map is shown further west than it is in reality.) Through the gate follow a faint path descending into Cwm Nantcol beneath the dark and solemn crags of Moelfre's east face. On reaching the lane turn right back to Cil-cychwyn.

Below: Rhinog Fach and Llyn Hywel from Y Llethr.
Opposite: Rhinog Fach and Llyn Hywel.

LLAWLECH AND PONT SCETHIN

When you take this long route into Ardudwy's mountains you will be walking through ancient history, for this kingdom has been well inhabited since Neolithic times and traces of prehistoric remains are still here on the ground. Although most modern-day traffic passes along the coast, before the nineteenth century engineers thought the space between the sands and the cliffs was too tight for a road. In those times the Welsh followed the old ways by heading inland over the mountain passes.

Tal y Bont lies on the Harlech road, a few miles north of Barmouth in the valley of the Afon Ysgethin. This pretty wooded valley starts you off in splendid fashion. An old drovers' road leads you to the ridge but not before showing you the faint remains of ancient cairns and stone circles.

Travellers of past times would have feared this journey and come prepared with guns and fast horses, for often thieves and highwaymen lay in wait. The name Bwlch y Rhiwgr (pass of the horns) gives the story away: the highwaymen's lookouts would sound their horns once the unwary travellers had passed, thus alerting the nearby band. Later in the day, beneath the slopes of Moelfre, you'll pass some innocent-looking ruins, little more than a lichenous pile of rubble. But these are the remains of an old coaching inn, where bandits once robbed a party of London gentlefolk who had halted here on their way to a society wedding at Harlech.

The mountain of Llawlech is the high point of the day. It too has a Bronze Age relic, an old cairn, probably marking a ritual site. From the drove roads and the ridges you'll come down to another ancient highway, the London to Harlech mail coach road, and this will take you into the valley where the old bridge of Pont Scethin takes it across the river. To the left and slightly down-valley is the rocky hill of Craig y Dinas. Perched on the top of this formidable rock was a huge pre-Roman fort, which was used by local chieftains until the thirteenth century for its strategic position overlooking the coast and guarding the mouth of the Ysgethin.

Opposite: The Ysgethin near Tal-y-bont.

LLAWLECH AND PONT SCETHIN

Within a stone's throw of the old highway is Cors y Gedol Hall, a sixteenth-century mansion built by the powerful baron Richard Vaughan. Although enlarged in later years into quite a sizeable estate, the original house and the gatehouse of 1630 remain intact and well worth seeing (permission is needed). Not far from the house is a Neolithic burial chamber, Coetan Arthur, where a 12ft/3.5m capstone leans against a cairn.

Distance 10 miles / 16km
Time 5½ hours
Ascent 2080ft / 635m
Technical difficulty •••
Strenuousness ••••
Map OS Explorer OL18 Harlech, Porthmadog
Start / finish Car park, Tal y Bont village
(GR SH 590218)
Public toilets At car park

1 From the back of the village car park head east along the tarred riverside path passing in front of Y Bedol Inn. Beyond the inn take the path into the woods of Coed Cors-y-gedol. Stay with the main path nearest the stream rather than taking the ones climbing left. Eventually this climbs out to a tarred lane next to a stone cottage, Llety-lloegr (the boarding house of the English), which was an old shoeing station and rest stop for drovers. From here you'll be following the drovers' route into the mountains.

2 By turning right along the lane you come to Pont Fadog, a fine one-arched bridge shaded by trees. The lane ends, to be replaced by two tracks. Take the right fork and follow the clear track over rough pastures to a nick in the ridge ahead – this is Bwlch y Rhiwgr. The nick turns out to be a narrow channel to the ridge, a good place for highwaymen to hide.

3 On reaching the top of the narrow pass climb left along the near side of the ridge wall and follow the meandering ridge to Llawlech's windswept summit. From the summit descend north along the grassy ridge with the ridge wall still to the right.

4 You eventually come down to a splendidly even grass track straddling a high unnamed pass. This is the old London to Harlech road. Turn left along it and descend northwards into the barren valley of Ysgethin. Although the monochrome green of the rushes and sedges seems a bit sullen when the sun's not out, the scene can be a bit of a chameleon. Late sun turns the paler vegetation into vibrant gold; I've never seen anywhere else quite like it.

Some way downhill along the track lies Janet Haigh's Memorial Stone, which was erected by her son Melvyn, Bishop of Winchester, after her death in 1953. It reads: 'To the enduring memory of Janet Haigh, who even as late as her eighty-fourth year despite dim sight and stiffened joints still loved to walk this way from Tal-y-Bont to Penmaenpool . . . Courage, traveller.'

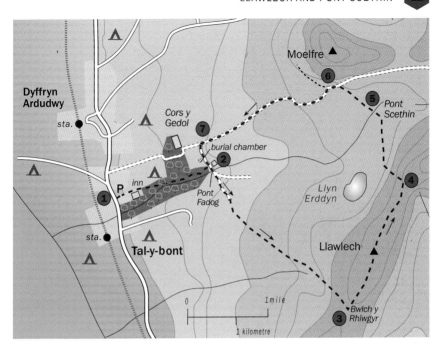

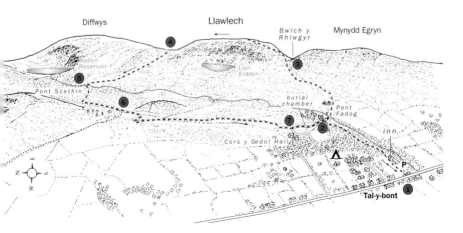

Above: Coetan Arthur, the burial mound near Cors y Gedol.
Opposite: Climbing out of the Ysgethin valley on the old mail coach road.

5 At the bottom the old highway angles left to cross Pont Scethin, an ancient one-arched bridge over the stream. The track, now a little less distinct, heads north-westwards to reach a stony reservoir road, where you turn left beneath the slopes of Moelfre. You'll see the ruins of the infamous Tynewydd Inn on the right beneath some conifers, while to the south lies the formidable rocky mound of Craig y Dinas.

6 There's a junction of tracks a short way beyond the conifers. Take the left fork, a stony track heading for a gate in a drystone wall before continuing across rough pasture-land towards the coast. At first there's a wall on the right, but beyond a sharp right turn the track becomes enclosed both sides by walls. It descends gradually towards the large complex of Cors y Gedol Hall.

7 Just before the hall turn left on a lane arcing back towards the Afon Ysgethin at Pont Fadog. The Coetan Arthur burial chamber is to your right. The track meets the outward route at Llety-lloegr. Descend on the path opposite the house into the woods of Coed Cors-y-gedol and follow it above the north bank of the stream to emerge by Y Bedol Inn at Tal-y-bont.

DINAS OLEU AND BARMOUTH

Barmouth lies at the foot of the Rhinogydd Mountains and looks out across the Irish Sea and the wide estuary of the Mawddach. Houses were built on steep hillsides overlooking the sands and most of the inhabitants were involved in fishing or shipbuilding. The town was also an important port. It has been suggested that during the Wars of the Roses Henry Tudor had intended to sail into Barmouth rather than Milford Haven, before engaging the troops of Richard III.

In a meeting of 1768 the shipmasters decided it was more expedient to have an English name inscribed on the sterns of their vessels – previously the town had been known as Y Bermo or Abermaw, the latter a shortened version of Abermawddach (the mouth of the Mawddach).

Around the turn of the nineteenth century tourism began, and the Barmouth seaside became an attraction for the gentry of the Midlands. The Cors y Gedol Hotel (now flats) was built in 1796 on what was then the beach. In 1798 the road from Dolgellau, which would form the High Street, was built, blasting through the rocks and borrowing ground from the beaches. This was followed by the railway, which crossed the Mawddach on a half-mile bridge with a swing section to allow shipping to pass.

Left: The promenade at Barmouth.

Tourism greatly increased as the early Victorians took to bathing and the sea airs, and hotels, boarding houses and shops shot up along the narrow plain. One visitor was William Wordsworth, who described the view across the estuary towards Cadair Idris as sublime and equal to any in Scotland. Charles Darwin, Lord Byron and Shelley also visited, along with the artists Turner and Richard Wilson, who came to capture the changing light and renowned beauty of the estuary and Cadair Idris.

The walk starts on the promenade, which was opened by former Prime Minister David Lloyd George in 1933. It continues along the quayside, where one of Barmouth's oldest houses, Ty Gwyn (the white house), was built in 1460. This stone-built hall house provided a safe meeting place for Henry Tudor's supporters during the Wars of the Roses; today it is a museum. Just behind it is the round house of Ty Crwn, built in 1834 as a lock-up jail for offenders waiting to be taken for trial at Dolgellau and a temporary hold for drunk and disorderly townsfolk.

The fine cliffs and crags of Dinas Oleu (the fortress of light) rise precipitously from the rooftops of old Y Bermo. In 1895 it became the first property donated to the National Trust. The benefactor, Mrs Fanny Talbot, was a friend to John Ruskin and two of the Trust's founder members, Octavia Hill and Canon Rawnsley. Narrow streets of the old town (Hen Bermo) take you on to the shoulder of Dinas Oleu where you'll find the Frenchman's Grave. This walled garden is the resting place of Auguste Guyard, a nineteenth-century French philosopher. After fleeing from the Siege of

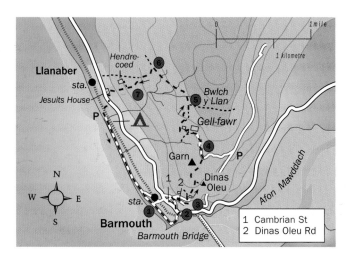

Paris he settled in one of Mrs Talbot's cottages in Barmouth. A keen horticulturalist, he cultivated rare herbs and trees on the poor soils of the hillslopes.

On the hills the walk passes the relics of ancient civilisations, including the hillfort Castell y Bermo. At first sight, crags and a substantial drystone wall obscure the fort's presence, but closer inspection reveals its square ramparts. Just before the final descent to the Jesuits' House, you can detour to see the remains of an old homestead and a Neolithic cairn.

Distance 5 miles / 8km
Time 3 hours
Ascent 1215ft / 370m
Technical difficulty ••
Strenuousness ••
Map OS Explorer OL18 Harlech or OL23 Cadair Idris
Start / finish Car park on Barmouth promenade (GR SH 614156)
Public toilets At car park

1 Head southwards along the promenade, following it round to the harbour area where you'll find the Sailors Institute, Ty Gwyn 'the Shipwreck Museum', Round House and the Lifeboat Museum. Views from the harbour are, as Wordsworth described them, sublime, with the cliffs and peaks of Cadair Idris seen across the bridge and the sandbars of the Mawddach Estuary. After going under the railway bridge turn left along Church Street, Barmouth's main shopping street, which later becomes Stryd Fawr (the big or 'high' street).

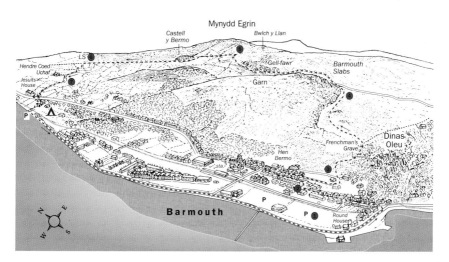

DINAS OLEU AND BARMOUTH

2 After turning right along the narrow Cambrian Street into the old town, turn right again at a crossroads to climb up Tan y Graig, which becomes Dinas Oleu Street where it veers right. A Dinas Oleu waymarker points you up the next narrow street, which rakes up the hillside. Take the lower right fork. Watch out for a path on the left, which takes the route between houses. It doubles back left to reach a patch of open green next to a viewing platform and indicator, where you can look down on the rooftops of the town and across the Mawddach Estuary out to sea.

3 Follow the clear, well-used path climbing the grassy hill slopes, and take the first right fork, a winding path that goes through a gate in a drystone wall. Make a there-and-back detour (right) along a slabbed path to the Frenchman's Grave, an enclosed garden and the resting place of Auguste Guyard.

After returning to the main path, follow it uphill with the wall to the right. Through another gate the path you want veers left heading towards the foot of the craggy Garn ridge. The path soon swings right to pass beneath this rough bouldery hillside. Beyond two more gates it tucks under the climbing crags known as the Slabs, where you can often see young climbers tackling the relatively easy rock routes. The path comes out on to a narrow tarred lane.

4 Turn left along the lane, which soon becomes unsurfaced with a pleasant grassy island up the middle. It winds up craggy hillside to the old stone-built farmhouse of Gellfawr. Follow the track between the farmhouse and outbuildings, ignoring the first way-marked track on the left but taking the second track on the left beyond the house and the last outbuilding. Beyond the trees the delightful grass track swings right by a wall and climbs beneath hillsides of grass and crag.

Take the waymarked left fork to pass between walls (not straight ahead through the gateway). The walls open out to an enclosed pasture, where the track follows the wall on the left before veering right to a stile by a gate. Follow another wall on the left – there are extensive rock outcrops on the other side – before veering away right and winding up the hillside to a stile by a gate in the top wall. A short way beyond the stile you meet the Bwlch y Llan path.

5 Turn left along this grass track, which curves half-right away from the wall. Over another stile by a gate the track comes to the remains of an incline used by the Hafotty manganese mines. Here the track passes to the right of the lower section of the incline towards a bouldery knoll. On closer inspection this is an ancient hillfort, Castell y Bermo, which was ultilised by the Romans; it's well worth while detouring to the top – it's a good lunch spot too.

6 On the left, rough hillside is soon replaced by farm pasture and the track comes to a ladder stile by a gate. Beyond the stile on the left there's a confusion of paths. Ignore the first gate and a ladder stile, both on the left, but go through the gateway just beyond them but still on the left. Now a walled grass track takes you down the hillside. At the next path junction, where there's a wooden pole and a mound of stones, turn left on a path enclosed by crumbling walls. Lower down, as the path descends towards the coast, you'll see a huge mound of boulders in the field to your right.

7 Go straight across a track from the buildings of Hendre-coed-uchaf (over on your right), then go straight ahead down a narrow field. At the bottom the path veers right. Turn left through a gate in the wall, descending towards a large stone building, the Jesuits' House (a spiritual retreat). The track turns left before this and comes out at the Barmouth to Harlech coast road.

Turn left along the road, then right along a signed tarred footpath descending beside cottages and past the town's campsite before crossing the railway. The path comes to a car park at the end of the promenade. At first substantial wooden groynes across the sands make a beach walk uncomfortable except when the tide is well out and you can round them, so possibly you'll be using the promenade for a return to the main car park, at least for a short way. Soon the sand creeps higher up those groynes making them scalable, and the bracing airs and the views across the Mawddach Estuary make this a pleasant ending.

Below: Dinas Oleu from the sands of Barmouth.
Overleaf: The view of Cadair Idris from Dinas Oleu.

TYRAU MAWR FROM CREGENNEN

High on a shelf beneath the northern cliffs of Cadair Idris's western ridges, and 800ft/244m above the village of Arthog and the waves of the Mawddach Estuary, lies Cregennen. As you stand by the shores of the twin Cregennen lakes at the start of the walk you're in the middle of one of Britain's great mountainscapes. To your left across the water is a bold rock peak with more attitude than altitude, but one that counterbalances the beautiful lakes and the majestic slopes of Cadair Idris.

Cregennen was formerly known as Crogenen, which comes from *crog-gangen*, the hanging branch. Historians believe that criminals from the ancient Welsh settlement of Llys Bradwen were hanged on a nearby tree.

The area around the lakes is of considerable interest to the naturalist and among the plant life you may find water lobelia, marsh St John's wort, marsh cinquefoil, quillwort and bogbean. The area was visited frequently by Charles Darwin, nineteenth-century author of *On the Origin of Species*. There are abundant fossils in the rocks here. The 705-acre/285-ha site is now under the protection of the National Trust.

This route will take you beneath Bryn Brith and along the shoreline of the lakes, so outside the winter months you can look for both aquatic and marsh-loving flora. The ridge will be remembered for stunning clifftop views, where it seems that the whole of Snowdonia – its mountains, its sands, its sweeping bays and its winding valleys – are laid out before you.

Tyrau Mawr (incorrectly spelled Tyrrau Mawr on current OS maps) means the great towers, and when you look from Cregennen up its northern ramparts to the pinnacles and crags you can see why. Once on top you are confronted with contrasting scenes. Towards Cyfrwy and Penygadair in the east the scenery is dominated by grey crags, cliffs and screes, but the ridges and hillslopes to the south are grassy with graceful arcs down into the valleys of Dysynni and Cadair. What follows is a joyous clifftop promenade, and it seems a pity when you finally have to come down.

Opposite: Approaching the Pony Path with Cyfrwy ahead.

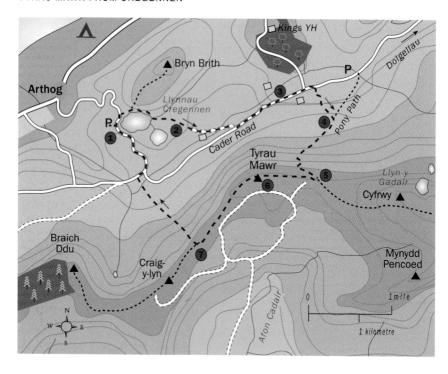

Distance 7 miles / 11.3km

Time 4 hours

Ascent 2080ft / 575m

Technical difficulty ••• (steep descent near the end)

Strenuousness •••

Map OS Explorer OL23 Cadair Idris

Start / finish Car park, Llynnau Cregennen (GR SH 658143)

Public toilets At car park

1 In all the majestic scenery at the start, you may think of abandoning a mountain walk and picnic instead on a nearby crag. Two coffees and a sandwich later though you'll be ready for a day on Cadair's western ridges.

Turn left out of the car park to follow the lane alongside the shores of the northern Cregennen Lake. A short way beyond a left-hand bend, turn right on a well-used path across rushy moorland. Ignore the left fork shortly beyond a stile, for this tackles Bryn Brith head on. Your route follows the lower, main path alongside the foot of the hill.

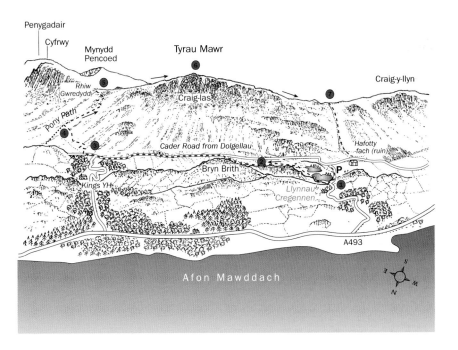

Penygadair
Cyfrwy
Mynydd
Pencoed
Tyrau Mawr
Craig-y-llyn
Rhiw
Gwredydd
Pony Path
Craig-las
Cader Road from Dolgellau
Hafotty
-fach (ruin)
Bryn Brith
Kings YH
Llynnau
Cregennen
P
A493
Afon Mawddach

Turn right at a path junction to continue parallel to the north-east shores of the lake and across heather to a stile allowing entrance into a large rough pasture.

2 Head slightly south of east to pick up a tractor track, which takes the route across high fields towards Nant-y-gwyrddail farm. Where the track turns right leave it and cross a ladder stile ahead. This takes the route above the farm to another stile. Beyond this turn left along the farm's drive, which leads through fields lined by gorse and bracken beneath partially wooded slopes scattered

with some quarry spoil. The track comes to a lane, Cader Road. On the other side of it grass slopes soar to the screes and crags of Tyrau Mawr. From here those crags seem to be overhanging. Turn left along the lane and follow it past the side-turning for Penmaen-pool and Kings Youth Hostel.

3 The path you want next isn't currently signed at the roadside. It starts beyond a gate on the right-hand side of the lane by some walled sheep enclosures. (A few paces further along the road, a gate on the opposite side is signed for Tynyceunant.)

TYRAU MAWR FROM CREGENNEN

Above the sheep enclosures the path goes through another gate and turns left. The path zigzags up the pastured hillside scattered with gorse, goes through a gap in the next wall, then angles south-south-east up the hillside with the Gwynant stream closing in on the right-hand side. The grass path climbs past weirdly wind-warped thorn trees before coming up to a ladder stile in a substantial wall. On the other side you join the main path to Cadair Idris, known as the Pony Path.

4 Turn right and climb the Pony Path, which eventually zigzags, sometimes with great slabs as a surface, to go through a gap in a wall, beyond which it reaches the col at Rhiw Gwredydd. Now you can see southwards into the deep grassy basin of the Cader Valley, where Cadair Idris displays its soft green side.

5 Most walkers will be turning left up the bouldery spur of Cyfrwy on their way to Penygadair, Cadair's highest summit, but your path turns right by the ridge fence to climb Tyrau Mawr. It passes the huge cairn and boulders on Carnedd Lwyd on its way to Tyrau Mawr's summit. From here you can look over those crags, cliffs, rock towers and gullies, down across the lakes of Cregennen to the Mawddach Estuary.

Opposite: Tyrau Mawr across Cregennen.
Above: On the path between Cregennen and the Cader Road.

6 The path down continues by the fence and exposed edge. Ignore the first stile in the fence and continue the descent to the saddle between Tyrau Mawr and the next peak, Craig-y-llyn.

7 A stile in the ridge fence here does mark the start of the path down. This is steep and uncompromising but it's quite safe and heads straight down grass slopes to the lane by the ruins of Hafotty-fach. There are ladder stiles in the cross-walls of the lower fields.

Turn right along the lane before turning left at the next junction. The new lane twists between low rock outcrops before coming to the northern Cregennen Lake and the car park.

CADAIR IDRIS:
THE CLASSIC CWM CAU CIRCULAR

Cadair Idris means the seat of Idris (Welsh for Arthur), but don't take the word seat too literally, for this isn't likely to have meant the throne of Idris. Some people believe that Idris refers to King Arthur or to the mythical Welsh giant of the same name. However, this Arthur is more likely to be the son of Meirion, who founded Meirionnydd; the area around Cadair was their seat or power base.

The northern cliffs of Cadair Idris rise out of the Mawddach Estuary in a series of stepped ridges: the first ones wooded with oak, as they have been since the last Ice Age; the second, a line of dolerite crags; and finally a long ridge fronted by cliffs, broken in the west and unyieldingly precipitous in the east. The cliffs are made up of granophyres, a particularly hard crystalline rock which has resisted erosion, while the softer rocks overlying it have been washed away. Indeed, the volcanoes and ice sheets of previous aeons have been kind to this great mountain range, shaping them into magnificent form. The Mawddach view was described by Wordsworth as 'sublime'. Charles Darwin, who spent much time here, wrote to his colleague Sir Joseph Hooker in 1869: 'Old Cader is a grand fellow and shows himself superbly with ever-changing light. Do come and see him.'

To the south of Cadair Idris is the valley of the Afon Dysynni, which flows south-westwards through the village of Abergynolwyn before being diverted from the fine green valley formed by the massive Bala Fault to squeeze into a narrow gorge between Foel Cae'rberllan and Gamallt. This happened in the last Ice Age, when the original line of the river was blocked by ice behind which a glacial lake formed. Eventually the river broke out along this new line.

Like Snowdon, Cadair Idris became popular with tourists during Victorian times and the coming of the railways. In the nineteenth century Richard Pugh, a Dolgellau

Opposite: Looking down one of Mynydd Pencoed's gulleys.

man, built a hut where an elderly lady served teas to the visitors brought up the mountain by local guides. Each morning the lady would be up at dawn and would hurry up the mountain with her wares. In 1871 Pugh's son guided the famous diarist Francis Kilvert up Cadair. Incessant rain didn't do much for Kilvert's mood; he wrote that this was 'the stoniest, dreariest, most desolate mountain I was ever on'.

The walk in this chapter will tackle the mountains at Cadair Idris's heart, including the highest, Penygadair, which rises to 2930ft/893m. It will take in the glacial corrie of Cwm Cau and the subsidiary peaks of Mynydd Pencoed and Mynydd Moel.

Most of the day will be spent in the Cadair Idris National Nature Reserve. In the early stages you'll see the carefully managed woodland that cloaks the southern slopes of Ystrad-gwyn, while in the fenced enclosures, away from grazing sheep, you'll see species such as bilberry and heather regenerating. Around the steeper ground of the rock outcrops where the sheep don't go, you may spot the delicate leafless stem and little white flowers of the starry saxifrage, or maybe the blue-purple globe-flowered devil's bit scabious. Both love the alkaline soils leached from the volcanic rocks. The whole journey is magnificently highlighted by the effects of volcanic activity, glaciation and the subsequent colonisation by flora.

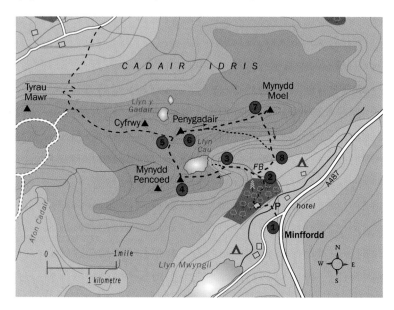

Distance 6 miles / 9.5km
Time 4 hours
Ascent 3130ft / 955m
Technical difficulty •••• (rugged mountain terrain)
Strenuousness ••••
Map OS Explorer OL23 Cadair Idris
Start / finish Car park, Minffordd (GR SH 732116)
Public toilets At car park

① Go through a kissing gate beyond the toilet block and on to a drive passing along an avenue of fine horse chestnut trees, before turning left to pass in front of the National Trust information centre at Ystradgwyn. Turn

right through a gate into woods of oak with some limes, rowans and beech. Beneath the canopy a series of steps and stone slabs climbs steeply, always with the boisterous white waters of Nant Cadair for company below you on the right.

② The path emerges from the woods into the entrance to Cwm Cau, with the scree slopes of Penygadair visible ahead. You can see the return route beyond the slate bridge over the stream. The Minffordd Path swings left into the heart of the cwm, but its lake, Llyn Cau, stays hidden behind grassy moraines left by the retreating glacier.

③ Where the path divides, take the left fork, climbing to the ridge. Llyn Cau comes

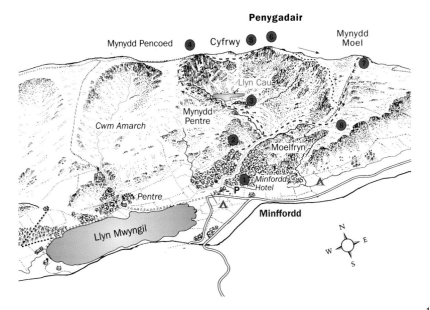

into view quite early in the climb, with the dark gullies and pillars of Craig Cau soaring from its waters. The ridge to Mynydd Pencoed's east summit above Craig Cau is a rocky one, but the path is always clear and offers views down to Llyn Mwyngil and the red screes of Graig Goch beyond. However, as you gain more height your attentions will be captured by the tremendous gullies that plummet down to Llyn Cau.

4 Mynydd Pencoed's bouldery east summit throws out two ridges – one above Cwm Amarch to its west summit and the other to the north, linking it with Penygadair. To your left the Pennant valley cuts through the softer side of Cadair's peaks, where most of the crag has been replaced by grass. The long ridges at the far side of the valley are Tyrau Mawr and Craig-y-llyn, hiding their sculpted northern crags and screes from view.

As you cross a summit ladder stile and descend north towards the col a distinctively shaped little hill with fine cliffs comes into view in mid-distance. This is Craig yr Aderyn (bird rock). Those cliffs used to rise from the sea and the flat fields below lay beneath a wide estuary. The sea has receded some four miles, but the cormorants still come to nest – it's their only European inland breeding site.

At the col a steep path, the Stone Shoot, comes up from Llyn Cau. From here the path up to Penygadair leaves the edge of the cwm to climb over rock outcrops. On gaining height it gradually arcs right.

5 The Pony Path route joins from the left and you find yourself looking down over the edge of another glacial corrie, with the lakes of Llyn y Gadair and Llyn Gafr far below. The serrated rock peak guarding the west side of the corrie is Cyfrwy, a climbers' favourite, and with its vast screes flowing down to the lake it packs a powerful presence.

Not far beyond the junction the path takes you through bouldery terrain to Penygadair's summit, where a leaky old stone hut, which provides a little shelter from the elements, lies just beneath the trig point. Cadair's great view is half-maritime, half-mountain. You cannot but be impressed by the sweep of Cardigan Bay, its long sands and its coastal marshes. It's all framed by the Llyn Peninsula, the great pointed peaks of central Snowdonia and the smoother Silurian hills of Mid Wales: mile upon mile of green ridge, anonymous hills which few walkers will be able to identify.

6 The onward route to Mynydd Moel begins with a simple but steepish descent east-north-east over bouldery terrain. This soon becomes a fine striding ridge with firm terrain of rock and grass. There are two parallel paths for much of the way, one for those who like to look over the edge, and one for others and for wintry conditions when the edge may not be all that clear. Not far before Mynydd Moel's summit, go over a ladder stile in a fence (not marked on current maps) which will guide you down the mountain.

The summit has a good-sized wind shelter not far from the precipices and a huge stony gully plummeting into lonely slopes interspersed with crag, heather and a tiny tarn, Llyn Arran.

7 The descent from the summit requires that you return to the fence you passed just before the final 100 metres of climb. You can either retrace your steps to the fence, short-cut to it by descending southwards, or follow the ridge path south-east, then cut off right on a narrow path over grass. The fence-side path is a fine grassy course at first and heads south-south-eastwards down the mountain.

The path now comes to a steep section. Here it becomes more eroded as it leaves the grass and descends into more friable terrain where scree and heather are introduced. The path of loose stones requires care to negotiate, but compensation comes with an exceptionally good view into Cwm Cau, highlighted by the cone-like face of Mynydd Pencoed and its dark rocks and pillars etched with the black shadows of two deep scree-strewn gullies. This view is depicted in Richard Wilson's 1765 painting of the mountain, which hangs in London's Tate Britain.

A path from the rim of Cwm Cau joins in from the right at a ladder stile and this co-incides with the worst of the erosion. Still lower down the path has been engineered with stone slabs. (I suspect that the slabs will soon advance up the steep eroded sections of the mountainside.)

8 Further downhill the path crosses the wall on the right and swings westwards through a grassy hollow between Mynydd Moel's low slopes and those of Moelfryn. It then descends further past a small forestry plantation to Nant Cadair. After crossing the slate footbridge over the stream and climbing the far banks you come to the outward route of the Minffordd Path. Turn left here and retrace the morning's route down through the woods, past the information centre and back to the car park.

Below: The entry into Cwm Cau.
Overleaf: Looking towards Penygadair from Mynydd Moel.

TARRENHENDRE FROM ABERGYNOLWYN

Abergynolwyn, which means the mouth of the river with a whirlpool, lies beneath the spruce trees cloaking the Tarren hills and the pastured foothills of Cadair Idris. The name came into being in the 1860s when the quarries of Bryn Eglwys, to which it is inextricably linked, expanded. Previously the settlement, with origins back to 1632, consisted of two hamlets, Pandy (mill), where the car park and café are now, and Cwrt (court) by the bridge over the Afon Dysynni.

Sited in Nant Gwernol, a wild valley delving deep into the Tarren hills, the Bryn Eglwys (church hill) Quarry had small beginnings under the ownership of an Aberdyfi man, John Pughe. The slate at this time was carried by packhorse on old drovers' roads to be exported from Aberdyfi. In 1864 William McConnel, a Manchester cotton mill owner, decided to diversify his interests as the American Civil War had made cotton supplies unreliable. He formed the Aberdyfi Slate Company and among his acquisitions were the leases to Bryn Eglwys.

Transportation of the slate was a real problem and the company made heavy investments to expand the quarry, including the building of seventy miners' houses in the village and the construction of a new narrow-gauge steam railway, the Talyllyn. The railway conveyed the slate to Tywyn, which by then was served by the Cambrian Coast Railway on the national railway network. The quarry faces themselves were high up the hillsides and needed horse-drawn tramways and inclines to carry the slate down to the valley.

Profitability was always questionable, both for the railway and the quarry. Although the local MP, Sir Haydn Jones, bought the leases and ran it for many years the quarry closed on Boxing Day, 1946. Fortunately for modern tourists, a preservation society was formed, and led by engineer and author Tom Rolt it brought the railway back from the brink, and even extended it to Nant Gwernol in 1976.

Opposite: On Tarrenhendre's summit.

TARRENHENDRE FROM ABERGYNOLWYN

Early in the day on your journey from Abergynolwyn's Pandy Square, you'll climb to the winding house of the Allt Wyllt incline and walk along the Galltymoelfre tramway to the next, the Cantrybedd incline. The trees of the forest have cloaked many of the features of Bryn Eglwys but you can see among the spoil heaps the remains of the barracks and the mill. In the hills themselves you'll escape the forestry and on the high ridges you'll be following in the path of pilgrims bound for Bardsey Island.

The attractive oakwoods of Dolgoch and their famous waterfalls make a fitting finale to the walk, and seekers of the perfect day out may well board one of the Talyllyn steam railway's little red carriages and travel in style back to Abergynolwyn.

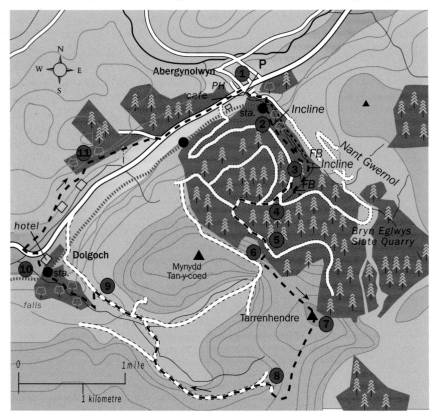

Distance 8¾ miles / 14.1km including the walk from Dolgoch back to Abergynolwyn
Time 5½ hours
Ascent 2360ft / 720m
Technical difficulty ••• (future forestry changes could make navigation more difficult)
Strenuousness ••••
Map OS Explorer OL23 Cadair Idris
Start / finish Car park, Abergynolwyn (GR SH 678069)
Public toilets At car park

1 A lane from the back of Pandy Square and its car park passes the modern building housing the café and some cottages before climbing above the last of Abergynolwyn's terraced houses into leafy Nant Gwernol. After a steep but short climb, leave the lane for a path on the right, signed to Nant Gwernol Station. This passes through deciduous woodland and follows the north-east bank of the lively Nant Gwernol. After going to the right over a footbridge the path comes to the station, which is the terminus of the narrow-gauge Talyllyn Railway. The route between here and point 3 will be highlighted by both yellow and blue waymarkers.

2 Turn immediately left, then left again at a T-junction of paths, to reach the restored winding house at the top of the Allt Wyllt incline. The small length of tram track helps the imagination picture the site in its heyday.

3 Beyond the incline the route continues through the forest to the Nant Moelfre stream and the foot of the Cantrybedd incline. Do not cross the footbridge here but continue with the path (signed with blue waymarks), which eventually doubles back right to climb to a flinty forestry road, where you turn left.

Down below you is the Bryn Eglwys Quarry. Slag heaps and the odd relic are still visible but the scene is being rapidly engulfed by the spruce trees. Even the great collapsed pit and its waterfalls are now concealed, as are some of the pulley houses I used to delight in photographing.

By now stands of spruce and larch have replaced the oaks and rowans but the forestry tracks take you quickly along the hill-sides in easy gradients.

4 Take the right fork forestry road, but then ignore another one doubling back right. The road you're on bends sharp left then sharp left again beneath the slopes of Foel Fawr.

5 You should leave the track when you reach a forestry vehicle lay-by on the left. By looking up to the skies on the right you should see a nick in the skyline. Your route to the top will climb to this. If you pass a wood cabin on the right-hand side of the forest road you've come about 50 yards/m too far.

Recent tree-felling has made what used to be an obvious route up a forest ride a little more difficult, but a couple of slate scree patches just to the right of Tarrenhendre's crags show the approximate direction. Higher up, the path enters a little gully before reaching the ridge near some sheep pens. If you look westwards down the other side you will be able to pick out a track in the valley. This will be used later in the day on the route to the Dolgoch Falls.

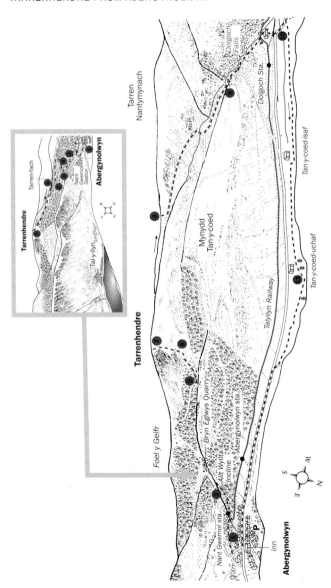

6 The climb to Tarrenhendre is now on extremely steep, grassy slopes to the left. Just follow the fence along the edge and above the forest and you'll arrive at the domed, grassy summit. In the south-west the Dyfi Estuary, which is often caught in a shimmering silvery light, leads the eye easily to the wide graceful curve of Cardigan Bay. You can trace the river through its wild inland meanderings to Pennal, beyond which it hides beneath afforested foothills. In the mid-distance on the southern horizon Pumlumon Fawr (Plynlimon) is the dominant mountain. Most eyes will be on Cadair Idris, however, for it is seen to splendid advantage, its angular craggy profile lording it over the hollow of the Dysynni Valley.

Below: Descending to Nant Dolgoch.

7 From the summit descend the south ridge alongside the fence. Below you and on the right you should be able to make out a track which gradually descends from the high slopes to the valley – this will be your route down. Where the ridge fence begins a gentle arc towards the right leave it and cut down grass slopes in a direction slightly south of west. This will bring you to the track-end. The track, in turn, leads to a more substantial grassy track passing beneath the sparse rocks of Tarren Nantymynach before descending towards the valley bottom.

8 At the next junction turn right on a track descending to ford the Dolgoch stream by some sheepfolds. It now heads north to

where a footbridge takes you across a side stream, Nant Sychnant. Turn left along the track on the other side and follow it through the main valley. The scenes are less wild with each footstep. From mosses and purple moor grass you pass through rough pastures with outcropping crags and some trees.

9 You now approach the woods of Dolgoch, with a fine waterfall coming down the craggy slopes of Pen Trum-gwr to their perimeter. You've two choices here. First you can continue along this track, which will stay above the woods and bring you out to the Abergynolwyn road just past the old quarry sidings of the Talyllyn railway. Secondly, and this is the better option, you can descend on a little path down into the woods. A step stile in the perimeter wall gives you entry to a path system which takes you past the impressive upper and lower Dolgoch Falls – the quickest route stays on the north-eastern side of the stream.

At the exit to the woods there's a donations box (remember this is a privately maintained path and not a right of way). The café and hotel lie to the right and there's a station on the Talyllyn railway line just above it. This narrow-gauge steam railway would take you in splendid fashion back to Nant Gwernol Station just beyond Abergynolwyn and is my recommended route of return. The following is for those who don't fancy the excitement of steam.

10 Turn left along the road beyond the hotel's car park. The road swings right to the opposite side of the valley. Where it turns left again leave it for a signed footpath over a stile. The path, waymarked in places, turns right and runs alongside the stream before angling and climbing very slightly left to a gate at the edge of woodland. With a fence on the right, a raised grassy causeway eventually passes above Tan-y-coed-isaf before dropping down right to pass through a gate to its front yard. Turn left through another waymarked gate and continue up the valley, this time passing above Tan-y-coed-uchaf. The path now climbs the hillside and passes through a gate into a plantation. The former path turned right here (and there's an old wooden signpost to this effect) but it is now overgrown and re-routed.

11 Follow the track further up the hill then turn right on a waymarked leafy track descending back towards the perimeter fence. The track comes out at a tarred lane from Rhiwerfa Farm. Turn right along it, back to the B-road. Follow this back to Abergynolwyn.

Opposite: A woodland path near the end of the walk.

MAESGLASE AND DINAS MAWDDWY

Dinas Mawddwy, at the start of the route, is a splendidly isolated village on the banks of the Afon Dyfi. Separated by a high pass, Bwlch Oerddrws, from Dolgellau and the main tourist trail, it's surrounded by the velvety green mountains of the Aran and the Dyfi – an idyllic centre for walking.

Today Dinas Mawddwy has a tranquillity about it, but it was not always so. In the middle of the nineteenth century, that famed traveller George Borrow walked through the village from Bala. In his book *Wild Wales* he noted that it was 'little more than a collection of huts . . . a squalid place'. He continued: 'I found it anything but silent and deserted. Fierce looking red-haired men, who seemed if they might be descendants of the red-haired banditti of old, were staggering about and sounds of drunken revelry echoed from the huts.' These, he later learned, were the hard-working, hard-drinking men of the local lead and slate mining fraternities, and not the infamous Red Robbers of Mawddwy (for more information, see the introduction to Walk 28).

Dinas was an important place in medieval times, with lead mines supporting a population of over a thousand. It was also an important cattle market, with many shops and a dozen public houses. Today, there is one public house and a hotel, but the last shop has closed. Many fairs were held each year. The village was until 1951 the terminus of a branch line from the main Cambrian Railway at Cemmaes Road. As well as passengers, the line used to carry slate from the Minllyn Mines, which can still be seen on the afforested hillside above the Buckley Pines Hotel. The old railway trackbed can be seen clearly by the campsite on the southern edge of town. Hereabouts you can also see Pont Minllyn, a fine seventeenth-century packhorse bridge.

Just down the road from the bridge, in a field called Maes y Camlan, a memorial stone has been erected to commemorate the battle of Camlan, in which King Arthur allegedly met his death after his forces were routed by those of Mordred.

Opposite: On the old miners' track climbing towards Bwlch Siglen.

Not far from Dinas is Maesglase, which would be more correctly spelled Maes-glasau, meaning the blue-green meadows, probably referring to the cwm of the same name rather than the mountain. It is the highest of the Dyfi hills. The top Maen Du, the black stone, was believed to be Maesglase's highest summit (2210ft/674m), but a recent survey showed a western outlier, Craig Rhiw-erch, to be higher at 2218ft/676m.

The approach through Cwm Maesglase is exquisite, with great contrasts between the meadows and hedgerows of the valley bottom and the harsher lines of the cliffs and waterfalls at its head. Old tracks take you past the sparse ruins of old slate quarries before zigzagging up to the pass of Bwlch Siglen. Gorse and bracken are soon replaced by heather, bilberry and a little cowberry as you make your way to the high ridges. Now a little path hugs the edge of the cliffs. The waterfall you saw earlier can be heard thundering down to the valley below long before you reach it. When you do you can almost feel the spray but be careful not to get too close to the edge – it's a long way down. Cadair Idris and Snowdon are clearly visible in an extensive summit panorama and, if the atmosphere is clear, then even the outlines of the Brecon Beacons and the Radnor Hills to the south will be added to the scene.

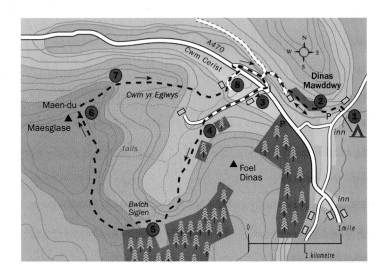

Distance 8 miles / 13km
Time 5½ hours
Ascent 2410ft / 735m
Technical difficulty ●●●
Strenuousness ●●●
Map OS Explorer OL23 Cadair Idris
Start / finish Car park, Dinas Mawddwy
village (GR SH 858149)
Public toilets At car park

1 Turn left out of the car park, following the Bala/Cwm Cywarch road out of the village. Turn left along the campsite drive then almost immediately fork right on a path climbing above the caravans on a long, narrow pasture. As you go through a large gate beneath trees don't be lured on to a track which continues on a level course across more fields. A few paces onwards, slant half-right on a faint path which climbs to a gate.

2 Through the gate turn left along a track by some woods. The track, lined by rhododendron bushes and at the base of a forestry plantation, heads westwards to pass above the cottage of Y Pentre, beyond which it descends to a narrow lane. Go straight ahead at the first junction before turning left at a T-junction. The lane now meets the main A470 road.

3 Another lane, staggered to the right on the opposite side of the busy road, takes the route past the cottages at Ffridd-gulcwm and into Cwm Maesglase.

4 Where the lane turns right and begins its descent towards the river, leave it for a left fork track through a gate. The soft greenness of the scenery is food for the soul and, as you continue along the track, there are increasingly wonderful views to the head of the valley where the slopes of Maesglase are interrupted by fine cliffs and waterfalls.

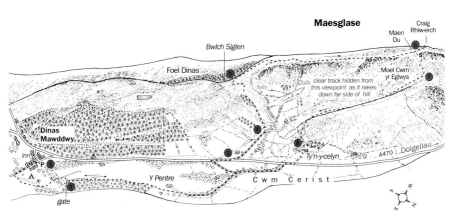

Above: Bwlch Siglen showing the path rising from below centre to the col.

The track gains height gradually as it tucks beneath the steep grass-and-bracken-cloaked flanks of Foel Dinas. After passing beneath some larchwoods and over a ladder stile beyond them, the track becomes rush-filled and it's better to follow a little path to left of the track, before continuing past the crumbling relics of old quarries. A slaty path continues the climb to the pass of Bwlch Siglen, which unkindly means the swamp pass. Here, the vast conifers of the Dyfi Forest sprawl southwards, relieved only by a few small pastures and felled stands.

5 From the col a narrow path winds up a spur of grass, bilberry and bracken, which lies to the left of a stream tumbling down the slopes. In its upper reaches, the path veers to the right away from the trees and across grassy moorland slopes. There's soon a slight descent towards a huge domed crag at the top of the falls, and the cliffs come back into view.

The path crosses the stream above those waterfalls – take a look down from the edge, but be careful, especially if it's windy. Continue along the path, staying quite close to the cliff-tops before climbing to the first, unnamed summit, which offers a great view into another glen, Cwm yr Eglwys (church corrie) – you'll see much more of this later. Here you turn left for the brief climb to the summit of Maen Du. Summit-baggers may want to do a there-and-back detour to the newly discovered highest point, Craig Rhiw-erch. Do this by following the ridge fence before veering right (west) to the small cairn on the main summit.

6 After returning to Maen Du, you have to try to find the little path marked on the OS maps as little black dashes, which zig-zag down the north-east ridge on a course to Moel Cwm yr Eglwys. This saves the very steep direct descent by the fence. To do this go over a step stile next to the summit fence corner and head north across heather. The faint path does come into view and winds down the north ridge before turning right across mine spoil back to the fence along the north-east ridge. Climb over the low fence (there's no stile) and veer left down the ridge.

7 A rush-lined track starts at the saddle just before the rise to Moel Cwm yr Eglwys (the hill of church valley). The track arcs around the north side of the pastured cwm, an offshoot of Cwm Maesglase, and eventually enters farm pastures and comes down to the farm at Ty'n-y-celyn.

Below: The view west from Maesglase over the ridges of the Dyfi Hills.

8 Go through a gate between the farmhouse and a barn, and turn left before continuing along the access drive to reach the busy A470 road. Cross the road, turn left for a short way using the grass verge, then turn right along a narrow country lane running parallel with the main road. You reach a junction with the outward route, where you should retrace your steps by taking the left fork lane then the right on a lane climbing beneath the slopes of Foel Benddin. An upper, left fork track takes you above the cottage of Y Pentre. Watch out for a gate on the right just before a metal gate across the track. This marks the start of a grassy footpath angling downhill towards a caravan site. The path meets a more prominent path, where you turn left, go through the lower (right) of two gates and then follow a hedge on the left before descending to the campsite drive near to its junction with the Dinas Mawddwy–Bala lane. Turn right along the lane, which passes through the village, to return to the car park.

ARAN FAWDDWY AND CWM CYWARCH

In the sixteenth century, Cwm Cywarch was home to the Red Robbers of Mawddwy, *Gwylliaid Cochion Mawddwy*. This band of thieves and murderers was feared throughout Wales and travellers would go miles out of their way to avoid conflict. The situation became so bad that Queen Mary herself commissioned the Sheriff of Meirionnydd, Baron Lewis Owen, to bring the men to justice, which he did with what some said was a vindictive zeal. On Christmas Eve 1553 eighty men were captured and mercilessly executed. But there would be revenge. Knowing the route the baron regularly took to the local assizes at Welshpool, the surviving robbers ambushed him at the ideal situation, Llidiart-y-Barwyn (the baron's gate), three miles west of Mallwyd, near Dinas Mawddwy. After felling trees to block his progress, the robbers greeted the baron and his men with a shower of arrows. The baron was dragged from his horse and stabbed to death. The remainder of the gang were then hunted down; most were executed but some fled the country.

Cwm Cywarch is completely rural today, but in times gone by it resounded to the sounds of lead mining. The Romans were the first to extract the metal but in the eighteenth century the veins were exploited by the powerful Mytton family. The mine closed in 1851 and many of its buildings were re-used by the farms – the house by the footbridge early in the walk was once the headquarters of the mining company.

At the head of the valley lies the tiny cottage of Bryn Hafod, now a mountaineering club hut for climbers tackling the great rocks of Craig Cywarch, which dominate the valley. In the 1960s legends such as Joe Brown and Chris Bonington came here and pioneered new routes to add to those of John Sumner, Barry Knox, Dave Adcock and the author of the area's first guidebook, R. E. Lambe.

The Aran's highest peak, Aran Fawddwy at 2969ft/905m, is also the highest Welsh peak south of Snowdon, and this shows in its panoramas, which extend to the Brecon Beacons in the south, the hazy foothills of the Marches in the east and Snowdon itself to the north.

Opposite: The verdant hollow of Hengwm.

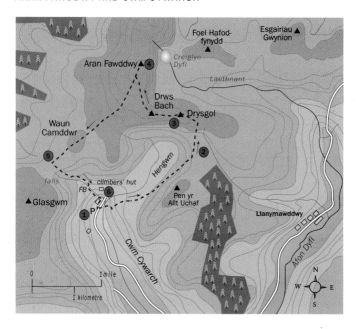

Distance 7½ miles / 12km
Time 4½ hours
Ascent 2640ft / 805m
Technical difficulty ●●● (high mountain terrain)
Strenuousness ●●●●
Map OS Explorer OL23 Cadair Idris
Start / finish Car park near end of Cwm Cywarch lane (GR SH 853187)
Public toilets None (nearest in Dinas Mawddwy)

1 From the car park turn left up the lane for a few paces, then turn right on a signed footpath enclosed by walls and shaded by hawthorns The track crosses a footbridge over the Afon Cywarch before climbing to open fields, where it continues towards the deep verdant hollow of Hengwm before raking across and up the slopes of Pen yr Allt Uchaf.

2 On reaching a marshy col at the head of the cwm, turn left on a path climbing roughly alongside a ridge fence to the summit of Drysgol. From here you look across to the tarn, Creiglyn Dyfi, and to the dark crags of Aran Fawddwy. The outflow of the lake, the infant Afon Dyfi (here known as the Llaethnant or milk stream), plummets down a narrow rocky gorge into a hollow beneath the grassy flanks of Foel Hafod-fynydd.

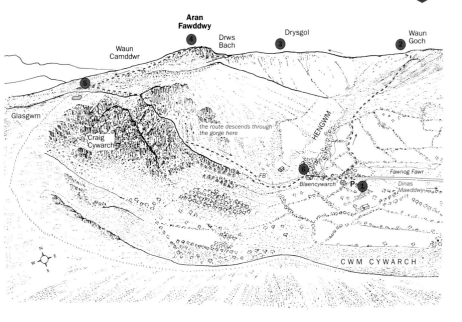

Aran
Fawddwy
④
Drws
Bach
Drysgol
③
Waun
Goch
②
Waun
Camddwr
⑤
Glasgwm
Craig
Cywarch
the route descends through
the gorge here
HENGWM
FB
⑥
Blaencywarch
P ①
Fawnog Fawr
Dinas
Mawddwy
CWM CYWARCH

Above: Creiglyn Dyfi seen from Drysgol.

3 Now the ridge rounds the head of Hengwm and becomes narrow and craggier. The path climbs along Drws Bach, where there's a memorial cairn to Mike Aspain, a member of RAF St Athan Mountain Rescue team, who was killed by lightning while on a call-out here in 1960.

Beyond this the path ascends the bouldery east slopes of Aran Fawddwy.

4 After climbing over a ladder stile you continue the climb past the cairn of the south summit and onwards across a bouldery ridge to the main summit's stone-built trig point.

Retrace your steps south-westwards along the ridge for about 400m. This time don't cross the ladder stile but continue south-westwards by the fence down broadening slopes of grass and rocky outcrops. The path continues over the slight bouldery hump of Waun Camddwr to arrive at a shallow boggy col beneath the rising slopes of Glasgwm.

5 Turn left at the col, past a couple of shallow pools and alongside another fence into a grassy upland cwm. As you descend, the buttresses of Craig Cywarch become more and more imposing on the right, while Gwaun y Llwyni's heathery slopes on the left have more broken crags and scree. A stream develops on your right and soon cuts itself a rocky gorge. Cywarch's crags grow ever more imposing as the path crosses a footbridge over the stream. The path now cuts itself a furrow through bracken-clad slopes.

6 The path comes to a stony track, which passes the farmhouse of Blaencywarch before reaching the lane-end. Follow the lane for the short way back to the car.

Above: On Aran Fawddwy's summit.
Opposite: Crossing the bridge over the Camddwr near the end of the walk.

ARENIG FAWR

Arenig Fawr rises southwards from the valley of the Tryweryn between Bala and Trawsfynydd. Its twin peaks feature predominantly in views from central Snowdonia and yet not that many walkers venture here, considering its 2800ft/854m altitude. In his 1862 book *Wild Wales* George Borrow wrote: 'Arenig is certainly barren enough, for there is neither tree nor shrub upon it, but there is something majestic in its huge bulk. Of all the hills which I saw in Wales none made a greater impression upon me.'

Today's Tryweryn valley is filled with the waters of Llyn Celyn but in the 1950s it was a wild upland valley with a village, Capel Celyn. This small, tightly knit, Welsh-speaking community included a school, post office, chapel and cemetery, and it was served by the Great Western Railway linking Bala with Trawsfynydd and Blaenau Ffestiniog. But post-war industrial England required new reservoirs – this time it was the Liverpool Corporation whose engineers turned their attention to Tryweryn. In spite of massive protests from the Welsh people, the British Parliament passed the bill in 1956. Thirty-five out of the thirty-six Welsh MPs voted against it, a decision thought to have led to the rise of Plaid Cymru, the Welsh Nationalist party.

The bulldozers moved in, the concrete dam was built and the village was demolished. The railway closed early in 1960, replaced by a new fast road from Bala to Trawsfynydd. The reservoir's opening ceremony was curtailed after just three minutes when protestors cut the microphone wires. But the waters rose above the old road and the bridge, and Capel Celyn became a dream of the past. In scant recompense, some of the stones from the original chapel were used in the construction of the new Memorial Chapel on the north shore of the lake; and in 2005 Liverpool Council apologised to the people of Wales for its part in the death of the valley community.

The railway trackbed is still useful for walkers; the car park lies on the site of the old Arenig station. Unfortunately, there are closed sections of track near some of the farms in the east, so the first mile uses the quiet Arenig Road instead.

Opposite: Looking across Llyn Arenig Fawr.

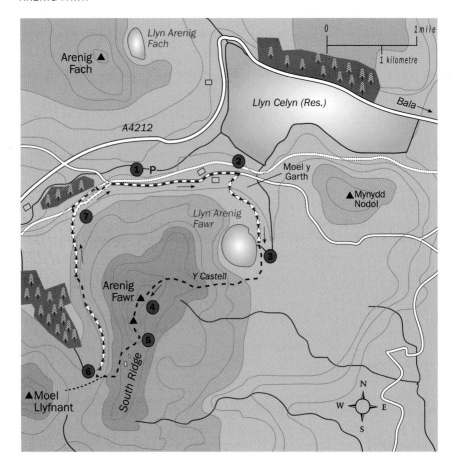

Distance 8¾ miles / 14.2km

Time 5 hours

Ascent 2180ft / 665m

Technical difficulty ••• (high mountain terrain)

Strenuousness •••

Map OS Explorer OL18 Harlech

Start / finish Arenig Station car park off the minor road to the south shore of Llyn Celyn (GR SH 830394)

Public toilets Nearest are in Cae-garnan car park on the west shore of Llyn Celyn (GR 845403), closed in winter months

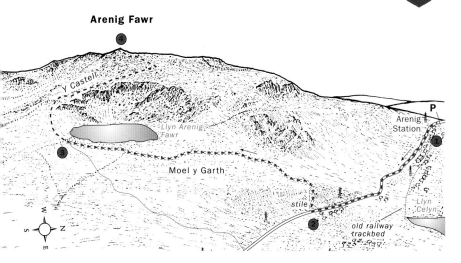

Arenig Fawr

Y Castell

Llyn Arenig Fawr

Arenig Station

P

Llyn Celyn

Moel y Garth

stile

old railway trackbed

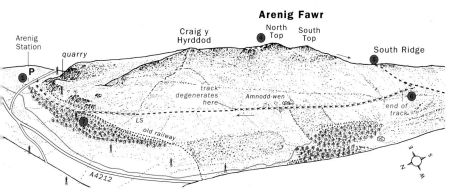

Arenig Fawr

Craig y Hyrddod

North Top

South Top

South Ridge

Arenig Station

quarry

P

track degenerates here

Amnodd-wen

end of track

LS

old railway

A4212

① Turn left out of the car park and follow the lane beneath the crags of the disused Arenig quarry, past a couple of farm houses and beneath a row of electricity pylons. Llyn Celyn comes into view across fields and the old railway track-bed.

② Watch out for a track leaving the road on the right at GR 846395, about a mile from the start – on your left you'll see a copse of trees surrounding the old railway track-bed. Recognised by a step-stile by a gate, the stone-and-grass track climbs the heather-and-bracken-clad western slopes of Moel y Garth. Soon Llyn Arenig Fawr comes into view. The squarish tarn is set in a grassy hollow beneath crag-fringed slopes, scraped with screes. The patchwork of heather and grass adds colour and mood, reflecting the seasons and the prevailing weather.

3 The track ends at Llyn Arenig Fawr's dam and sluice-gate. Cross its outflow stream, which can be difficult after snow-melt and periods of rain. In such times many walkers brave an iron ladder precariously spanning the water. Continue past a stone-built bothy on a narrow path veering right to climb the grassy spur of Y Castell (the castle).

At the top of the spur the scenery changes, with the cliffs, crags and scree being replaced by a mountainscape of grass and boulders. Arenig Fawr's summit appears for the first time on the left-hand side of the skyline. The path swings left in its direction, traversing its high eastern slopes before fading on the bouldery summit slopes. Now there's one final push over rock and grass to the summit wind shelter and trig point.

Within the wind shelter is a memorial plaque to the eight crewmen of a US Air Force B17 Flying Fortress, who died in 1943 when they crashed in thick fog into the crags just below the summit. It has also been said that Welsh painter James Innes, who had been renting a cottage with fellow Welsh painter Augustus John, buried some love letters here on his favourite mountain top.

The views from Arenig Fawr are some of the most extensive in Snowdonia, due to its relative isolation from the other major peaks. The western view is dominated by Moel Llyfnant's huge grassy massif but over its shoulder you can see the Rhinogydd mountains and their roller-coaster ridges. To the north Snowdon rises behind the rugged Moelwynion and Manod peaks, while the southern panorama includes those of the Aran and Cadair Idris.

4 Descend south along the ridge-fence before climbing to the rocks of Arenig Fawr's south peak. From here descend steepish slopes with the fence on your right. The South Ridge ahead is much lower and less well defined, with rocky tors and shallow tarns scattered across peaty grassland.

A fence will act as a guide for the first part of this ridge, but not far past the first of the lakes it leaves the ridge, descending to traverse the high western slopes. So keep to the narrow path on the west side of the ridge.

5 This eventually arcs right to rejoin the fence at a primitive stile (GR 824355). Beyond this a faint path descends grass slopes towards the damp, mossy saddle beneath Moel Llyfnant. Just before reaching the bottom look out for an equally faint path on the right. This will lead you to the end of a track, which will take you back to base.

6 The track is beautifully grassy at first and leads you in fine fashion beneath Arenig Fawr's west slopes. But beyond the ruins of Amnodd-wen farm it degenerates into a marshy rush-filled hollow, and for a short distance you'll be climbing slightly right to search for a drier footing. After the crossing of Nant Goch, on the slopes of Waun Goch the track becomes reasonably dry again and swings right as it approaches the grassy track-bed of the old railway.

Above: Looking south along the Arenig ridge from the main summit.

(7) Waymarks show you the way left down to the track-bed, which should be followed north-east with conifers to the left. A white arrow points to the right as the track becomes impassable and choked with scrub woods. Here you join a stony vehicle track just short of the Arenig Road, where you turn right back to the car park.

ABOVE BALA

Bala, which means outflow of the lake (a reference to the nearby Llyn Tegid), is a lively old market town dominated by a wide main street (Stryd Fawr), lined by cafés, gift shops and inns. It soon becomes obvious that it has religious roots, for besides the number of chapels there are two statues: one of Dr Lewis Edwards, founder of the Methodist College and, opposite the White Lion, another of Rev. Thomas Charles, a founder of the British and Foreign Bible Society.

The Society started as a result of one poor girl's dedication. As a teenager Mary Jones longed for her own Bible. Though she had no shoes she trekked across the hills from her home in Llanfihangel-y-pennant beneath Cadair Idris to Bala, a distance of 30 miles/48 km. Rev. Thomas Charles had no Bibles to sell but, inspired by her persistence, he gave her his own.

There are also two old fortresses. Tomen y Bala lies in the heart of the town behind the main street. First occupied by the Romans, this 30ft/9m mound, 130ft/40m in diameter, has a hedge and a tree on the top but in the early thirteenth century it was a powerful fortification held by Llewelyn ap Ioworth (Llewelyn the Great). At the other end of town by the station of the Bala Lake Railway, the other remains are of a Norman motte-and-bailey castle.

Bala's growth coincided with that of the local woollen industry, and the town was noted for its stockings. Thomas Pennant came here in 1786 and painted a fascinating picture of life in the town: 'Round the place, women and children are in full employ, knitting along the roads; and mixed with them Herculean figures appear, assisting their Omphales in this effeminate employ.' (Omphale was a Queen of Lydia to whom Hercules was enslaved as one of his twelve labours.)

Bala's lake, Llyn Tegid (the lake of beauty), is the largest natural lake in Wales at 4 miles/6.4 km long by ⅔ mile/1 km wide; it was formed in the last Ice Age some 10,000 years ago. The gwyniad, a freshwater whitefish, was trapped in the lake at

Opposite: Bala seen from the slopes of Mynydd Cefn-ddwy-graig.

this time, and it's the only place where it can be found. Unfortunately, deteriorating water quality and the introduction of another fish, the Eurasian ruffe, which eats its eggs, has endangered the species. As a result, conservationists have transferred some of their eggs to another lake nearby.

The walk goes over the bridge at the north end of the lake quite early and you'll notice the fine-looking conical peak, Aran Benllyn, which gets its name from Penllyn, part of Bala. Over the bridge you come to the terminus of the Bala Lake Railway, one of those fascinating narrow-gauge steam railways for which Wales is famous. Trains run to here from the main station at Llanuwchllyn, a village on the south-west shore of the lake, on the track-bed of what used to be the Great Western Railway's Ruabon–Barmouth line.

Views of both lake and town are superb as the route climbs past bluebell woods on to the hillsides beyond. It's quite likely that sailing boats and windsurfers will be enjoying Tegid's breeze-ruffled waters, and soon Arenig Fawr appears beyond foothills to the north of the lake. Too soon the path leaves the hills to return to Bala, but those views will stay with you.

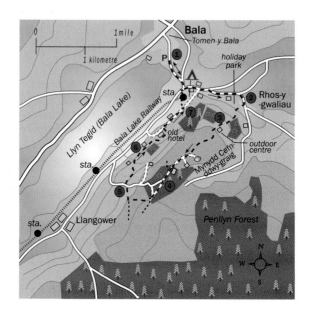

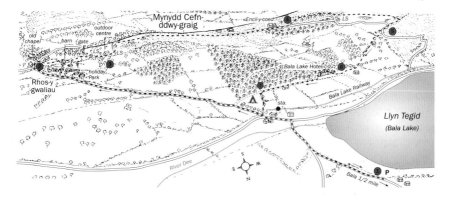

Distance 4½ miles / 7.2km
Time 3 hours
Ascent 790ft / 240m
Technical difficulty •
Strenuousness •
Map OS Explorer OL18 Harlech
Start / finish Car park on Heol Tegid (Bala St) past last houses at the north-east end of Llyn Tegid (GR SH 928355)
Public toilets Nearest ½ mile / 0.8km to west, near lakeside Sports Centre and Lake Warden's Office

1 From the car park turn right along the road, which joins the B4391. Follow this over the bridge which spans the outflow of Llyn Tegid. Ignore the right turn-off around the lake but instead pass the Pen y Bont camp-site. Take a right-fork lane signed to Rhos y Gwaliau.

2 Turn right into Rhos y Gwaliau village. The footpath required now begins opposite an old chapel (GR 944347). Through a gate it heads south-west on a sunken grass track across a field. To your right here you'll see the chalets of the Pen y Garth holiday park. Turn off this track by an old barn, bearing left to climb a sloping field to a metal gate beneath some trees. A waymark arrow highlights a leafy path continuing uphill alongside a small dyke on the left.

3 Go over a ladder stile at the brow of a slope, then follow a grass path passing to the right of the outdoor activities centre. At the far end of the complex a gate gives access to an enclosed grass path.

Go over the next ladder stile on to the open hillside. A marshy path climbs by the wall on the left before doubling back right on to the crest of the moor, which is interspersed with gorse and crag. The path becomes more of a sheep track and is easily lost; if in doubt stay with the crest which leads you south-west. If misty conditions prevail, an alternative would be to stay close to a fence on the left side of the crest. Except for one short stretch, where it detours a short way downhill, this fence will guide you to a well-defined track by an anglers' tarn. The crest path would rejoin you here and continues to the plantation of Cefn-ddwygraig, which was completely clear-felled around 2005, but has since been replanted with birch and conifers.

A tarred road begins at the forest's edge where it passes the whitewashed cottage of Encil y Coed.

4 To save walking on too much tarmac, leave the road for a narrow, grassy forestry track forking left. On meeting another track take the left fork, then turn right at a waymark arrow to cross a ladder stile on to a high hillside pasture. Follow a sunken grass track for a few yards but leave it for a very faint track angling half-right to descend to the bridleway track at the bottom of the field. Turn right along this and follow it back to a high, tarred road (the same one as you left beyond Encil y Coed).

5 Turn left to descend along the road for a few paces then turn right along a signed footpath across high moor. The faint path heads roughly northwards across hill-slopes of grass and bracken. It nears a fence on the right at one point before arcing left on nearing some trees, to join a lower path veering right to a gate.

Through the gate a clear path continues across meadows beneath trees, and crosses a little stream by a shaded cottage on the left. It continues with a fence on the left to pass the cottages at Graienyn, beyond which it passes beneath fine mixed woodland fringing a golf course.

6 Over a stile the route turns right along a stony track to the former Bala Lake Hotel, which is currently a Civil Service retreat. Turn right, then left (as signed) to pass through the complex and continue along a stony track with farmland on the left and woodland on the right.

7 After passing a recently renovated stone-built house, continue along the road until you see a gate on the left at the edge of the next field. Go through this and follow the hedge on the left across two fields before crossing the track of the Bala Lake Railway on a splendid railway footbridge. Pass to the right of the railway's office to come to the road. Turn right then left over the bridge back to the car park.

Opposite: Bala seen from the descent from Mynydd Cefn-ddwy-graig.
Overleaf: Descending towards Llyn Tegid with Arenig Fawr on the horizon.

APPENDICES

Maps

Ordnance Survey Explorer (1:25,000)
OL17 Snowdonia: Snowdon/Yr Wyddfa
OL18 Snowdonia: Harlech, Porthmadog,
　Bala
OL23 Snowdonia: Cadair Idris & Llyn Tegid

Ordnance Survey Landranger (1:50,000)
Sheet 116 Snowdon
Sheet 124 Porthmadog & Dolgellau
Sheet 125 Bala & Lake Vyrnwy

Harvey Superwalker Maps (1:25,000)
Snowdonia Cadair Idris
Snowdonia Aran
Snowdon and the Moelwynion
The Glyderau and the Carneddau
Rhinogs (Rhinogydd)

Harvey British Mountain Maps (1:40,000)
Snowdonia
Snowdonia South

Public transport

Buses
Sherpa Buses run regularly around the
heart of Snowdonia between Caernarfon,
Llanberis, Betws y Coed, Beddgelert,
Capel Curig and Conwy and these are
supplemented by a fairly good network
run by Express Coaches, Arriva and Lloyd's
of Machynlleth.

　Bus timetables for Gwynedd (high
Snowdonia including the Cadair Idris and
Bala areas) can be obtained from Tourist
Information Centres (TICs) or can be
accessed and downloaded at the website
www.gwynedd.gov.uk/bwsgwynedd.
(Unless you read Welsh you'll have to
change the language to English – the link
is at the top right of the web page.)

　Timetables for the Conwy region, which
includes Penmachno, Dolwyddelan and
Betws y Coed, are available twice a year,
either from Tourist Information Centres or
by sending a 9 x 6in stamped addressed
envelope to:
　　Conwy County Borough Council
　　Public Transport Section
　　Highways & Transportation Department
　　The Heath
　　Llanfairfechan LL33 0PF

Trains

There's a mainline railway linking Llandudno, Betws-y-Coed and Blaenau Ffestiniog – useful for routes around Dolwyddelan and on the Moelwynion range. The Cambrian Coast line from Pwllheli calls at Porthmadog, Talsarnau, Harlech, Llanbedr, Talybont, Llanaber and Barmouth (good for the Rhinogydd). The narrow-gauge Welsh Highland Railway runs from Caernarfon to Porthmadog and is useful for Snowdon, Mynydd Mawr and the Moel Hebog ridges, calling at Waunfawr, Rhyd Ddu and Beddgelert. Another narrow-gauge railway, the Ffestiniog Railway from Porthmadog to Blaenau Ffestiniog via Tanygrisiau, is excellent for the Moelwynion and Manod peaks. Websites:

www.nationalrail.co.uk

www.traveline-cymru.org.uk

Best bases

BALA is central for much of the region and has a good deal of accommodation ranging from a private hostel and several campsites through to fine hotels and country houses. It has a small outdoor gear shop, and a couple of small supermarkets.

Tourist Information Centre: Bala
Telephone 01678 521021
Email: bala.tic@gwynedd.gov.uk

BANGOR This pleasant university city on the shores of the Menai Straits has good accommodation and speedy road links to Aber and Llanfairfechan, the resorts best placed for routes into the northern Carneddau. There are plenty of shops and supermarkets.

Tourist Information Centre: Bangor
Telephone 01248 352786
Email: bangor.tic@gwynedd.gov.uk

BARMOUTH A lively seaside resort with plentiful accommodation, including hotels of all grades, B&Bs and a campsite. Barmouth is very handy for the southern Rhinogydd ridges, from Garn to Diffwys (south peak). There is only one outdoor gear shop, but otherwise the shopping is good and includes a large supermarket.

Tourist Information Centre: Barmouth
Telephone 01341 280787
Email: barmouth.tic@gwynedd.gov.uk

BEDDGELERT Beautifully situated at the confluence of the Colwyn and the Glaslyn and beneath the more verdant and sylvan slopes of Snowdon. Beddgelert, with its twin-arched bridge and pretty stone cottages, makes an ideal base for the Nantgwynant Hills, including Moel Meirch and Ysgafell Wen. There are a couple of campsites and very high-standard country house hotels and several B&Bs. Walkers can tackle Moel Dyniewyd and Mynydd Sygun from the village.

Tourist Information Centre: Beddgelert
Telephone 01766 890615
Email: tic.beddgelert@eryri-npa.gov.uk

BETWS Y COED Pronounced something like 'bettuz ee koyd', this large and bustling village is set by an equally bustling river, the Llugwy, not far from its confluence with the Afon Conwy. Betws has scores of B&Bs and many hotels. It's a good place for renewing supplies, with a choice of grocers, bakers and several gear shops.

> Tourist Information Centre: Betws y Coed
> Telephone 01690 710426
> Email: tic.byc@eryri-npa.gov.uk

CAERNARFON This is a fine place to stay with its castle, town walls and historic streets. There is good accommodation, including hotels, inns, B&Bs and several campsites. The excellent bus services mean that, although distant from the big hills, the walker can plan quite flexible walks including linear routes. There are scores of shops and lots of cafés.

> Tourist Information Centre: Caernarfon
> Telephone 01286 672232
> Email: caernarfon.tic@gwynedd.gov.uk

CAPEL CURIG This linear village straddles the A5 in small huddles of cottages for about three miles. Capel Curig has a few good hotels and B&Bs, a youth hostel and a campsite. There are a couple of outdoor gear shops too. The Pinnacle Café at the junction of the A5 and the A4088 is a meeting place for many walkers and climbers before and after their forays into the mountains. It is well placed for routes on the southern Carneddau and the Glyderau.

CONWY Sited between the Carneddau's northern reaches and the sea, with town walls, a castle by the fishing harbour and a modern marina, Conwy offers walkers a chance to relax in fascinating surroundings after they've had a day on the hills. Walkers can step out of their B&Bs straight on to Conwy Mountain. The town offers a wide variety of accommodation, including hotels, B&Bs and caravan sites (no campsites – the nearest is at Dwygyfylchi).

> Tourist Information Centre: Conwy
> Telephone 01492 592248
> Email: conwy@nwtic.com

DOLGELLAU Although it is sited beneath Cadair Idris some way south of the region, Dolgellau is reasonably placed for the southern Arenig peaks. The charming country town built from stone and slate has plentiful accommodation, including hotels and B&Bs. It is also well served by public transport.

> Tourist Information Centre: Dolgellau
> Telephone 01341 422888
> Email: tic.dolgellau@eryri-npa.gov.uk

HARLECH This pretty castle-crowned town has a small amount of accommodation, B&Bs and hotels. There are many smaller villages nearby, including Talsarnau and Llandanwg, with more accommodation, as well as large coastal campsites, but only a limited number of shops.

> Tourist Information Centre: Harlech
> Telephone 01766 780658
> Email: tic.harlech@eryri-npa.gov.uk

LLANBEDR This small village between Harlech and Barmouth is known as a walkers' centre although the youth hostel is now closed. It can offer a couple of shops, a couple of inns and nearby campsites.

LLANBERIS Snowdonia's biggest mountain village has small and large hotels, B&Bs, cafés and varied shops. Pete's Eats has been described as 'the best chippy in the world'. The large and lively village is handily placed for the Llanberis Pass routes up the Glyderau. NANT PERIS, its smaller neighbour, has a pub and two campsites catering mainly for tents.

Tourist Information Centre: Dolgellau
Telephone 01286 870765
Email: Llanberis.tic@gwynedd.gov.uk

LLANFAIRFECHAN The Victorian resort of Llanfairfechan hasn't as much accommodation as it had in the past, but there are a few B&Bs scattered around, along with a couple of cafés on the promenade and a handful of shops.

LLANRWST This attractive riverside market town has a couple of hotels, a campsite and a few B&Bs. There are takeaways and cafés as well as a good variety of shops.

MACHYNLLETH While it's to the south of the area and a couple of miles outside Snowdonia on the banks of the Dyfi river, Machynlleth has good transport links and is well placed for the southern Tarren hills and is not far from the Dyfi Hills. It's a lively if small market town with plenty of shops – some quite unusual ones, too. There are many hotels and B&Bs.

MAENTWROG This very pretty village overlooks the verdant Vale of Ffestiniog and has an inn, a hotel and a couple of B&Bs. It is handy for the northern Rhinogydd as is the nearby hamlet of Gellilydan, which has a caravan club campsite and a good pub.

NANTGWYNANT This tiny hamlet of a few cottages, a youth hostel (Bryn Gwynant) and campsite is set among the stunning scenery of the Glaslyn Valley between the lakes of Dinas and Gwynant. It's a good base for explorations of Moel Meirch, Ysgafell Wen, Craig Llyn-llagi and Cnicht and only a short bus ride away from start points for Moel Siabod.

PENMAENMAWR / DWYGYFYLCHI A seaside resort dating from Victorian times, Penmaenmawr town has been a bit down-at-heel, not helped by the modern A55 expressway which has tourists speeding by without a second glance. Things have improved recently, and the town is very handily placed for an exploration of Tal y Fan and its ancient circles and burial mounds.

Dwygyfylchi is set in a pleasant pastoral hollow between the coast and the Sychnant Pass, and is ideally placed for Tal y Fan and Conwy Mountain.

Together, the two resorts have a campsite, a caravan site, B&B's, inns and a few shops.

PORTHMADOG This busy resort sited at the mouth of the Glaslyn Estuary has accommodation to suit all tastes, ranging from hotels – including a Travelodge – to B&Bs and campsites. There is a large supermarket, several cafés and many specialist shops.

Nearby TREMADOG, a climbers' centre, has a few inns, a fish-and-chip shop and a village store. The well-known climber Eric Jones runs a café, bunkbarn and a campsite for tents – all just east of Tremadog (telephone 01766 512199).

Tourist Information Centre: Porthmadog
Telephone 01766 512981
Email: Porthmadog.tic@gwynedd.gov.uk

ROWEN Little Rowen, which lies in a pastoral hollow between the foothills of the Carneddau and the Conwy Valley, is chocolate-box pretty, with whitewashed cottages, teahouses and rose gardens. It has an excellent pub, a couple of very fine country house hotels and a youth hostel, which is a mile or so uphill towards Tal y Fan. The village is a lovely out-of-the-way find, and is great for explorations deep into the Northern Carneddau.

TYWYN Although well sited and reasonably provided with shops, hotels and B&Bs, Tywyn is suffering in the same way as many of Britain's Victorian seaside resorts due to a lack of long-stay visitors. As a result it's a little dog-eared in places. However, it's nice to take in the sea air after a day on the mountains, and there are good transport links for walks on the peaks of both Cadair Idris and the Tarren.

Tourist Information Centre: Tywyn
Telephone 01654 710070
Email: Tywyn.tic.gwynedd.gov.uk

Youth hostels

There are many youth hostels in Snowdonia but, beware, it is a fast-diminishing list. For the latest available, contact:

The YHA National Office
Trevelyan House
Dimple Road
Matlock
Derbyshire DE4 3YH
Telephone 0870 770 8868
Website: www.yha.org.uk

Other websites

Welsh Tourist Board
www.visitwales.com
Snowdonia Information
www.visitsnowdonia.info
Accommodation
www.4tourism.com
Campsites
www.ukcampsite.co.uk
Independent hostels
www.hostels.com/wales

The Welsh language

Some Welsh words

Aber	river mouth	Esgair	ridge
Afon	river	Eryri	eagles' abode
Arddu	black crag	Fawr/mawr	large
Bach/fach	small	Felin/melin	mill
Bedd	grave	Ffordd	road
Betws	chapel	Ffynnon	spring
Blaen	head of valley	Ffridd	enclosed grazing land
Bont/pont	bridge	Glas/las	blue
Bwlch	pass	Gwrydd	green
bws	bus	Gwyn	white
Cae	field	Gwynt	wind
Caer	fort	Hafod	high-altitude summer dwelling
Carn/carnedd/garn/garnedd	cairn/cairns	Hendre	winter dwelling
Capel	chapel	Isaf	lower
Carreg/garreg	stone	Llan	church or blessed place
Castell	castle	Llwybr cyhoeddus	public footpath
Cefn	ridge	Llwyd	grey
Cors/gors	bog	Llyn	lake
Clogwyn	cliff	Maen	stone
Coch/goch	red	Maes	field/meadow
Coeden/coed	tree/wood	Melyn	yellow
Craig	crag	Moch	pig
Crib	sharp ridge	Moel/foel	featureless hill
Cwm	coomb	Mynydd	mountain
Cwn	dog	Nant	stream
Cymru/Cymraeg	Wales/Welsh	Ogof	cave
Dinas	hill fort (or town)	Pant	clearing, hollow
Diolch	thank you	Pen	peak
Du/ddu	black	Person	cascade
Drum/trum	ridge	Plas	mansion
Drws	door	Pwll	pool
Dyffryn	valley	Rhaeadr	waterfall
Dwr	water	Rhyd	ford
Eglwys	church	Saeth(au)	arrow(s)

THE WELSH LANGUAGE

Troed	foot of
Twll	hole, fracture, broken
Ty	house
Uchaf	high, higher
Waun	moor
Wen	white
Wrach	witch
Y, Yr	the
Ynys	island

Pronunciation of consonants

c   always hard, like the English 'k', thus
coed = 'koyd'

ch   as in the Scottish 'loch'

dda voiced 'th' as in 'booth'

f   like the English 'v', thus fach = 'vach'

ff   like the English 'f'

ll   a Scots 'ch' followed by an 'l' (blow air
out between your tongue and your top
teeth when pronouncing)

Pronunciation of vowels

w   can be a consonant or a vowel. When
working as a vowel, pronounced like
'oo' as in 'cook' or 'moon'.

y   can be a consonant or a vowel. When
working as a vowel, pronounced like
'i' as in pin or 'ee' as in 'seen'.

u   exactly the same.

The letters j, k, q, v, x and z are not used in
true Welsh words.